Keto Slow Cooker Cookbook for Beginners:

150 Wholesome Low-Carb Recipes. Elevate Your Ketogenic Lifestyle with Quick Nutrient-packed Meals

Table of contents

Mastering the Keto Diet..7

What to Eat and Avoid for Success..10

Tips for Effective Slow Cooking..15

BREAKFAST...**17**

Keto Slow Cooker Spinach and Feta Frittata...18

Low-Carb Blueberry Lemon Breakfast Cake...18

Slow Cooked Spicy Sausage and Egg Casserole..19

Crockpot Pumpkin Spice Latte Oatmeal...19

Bacon and Mushroom Keto Quiche...20

Slow Cooker Cheesy Avocado Breakfast Casserole.......................................20

Crockpot Cinnamon Almond Breakfast Porridge..21

Slow Cooker Sausage and Peppers Breakfast Hash.......................................21

Crockpot Vanilla Bean and Berry Compote..22

Slow Cooker Mexican Breakfast Casserole...22

Keto Crockpot Chorizo and Egg Scramble..23

Crockpot Coconut Cream and Nut Granola...23

Slow Cooker Bacon and Egg Stuffed Peppers...24

Keto Crockpot French Toast Casserole..24

Slow Cooker Spinach and Mushroom Breakfast Quiche...............................25

LUNCH..**27**

Slow Cooker Buffalo Chicken Lettuce Wraps..28

Keto Beef Taco Soup..28

Creamy Cauliflower Bacon Soup...29

Crockpot Jalapeño Popper Chicken Salad...29

Slow Cooked Zucchini Lasagna...30

Crockpot Keto Chicken Caesar Salad..30

Slow Cooker Creamy Tomato Basil Soup..31

Crockpot Lemon Thyme Chicken Soup...31

Keto Slow Cooker Pulled Pork Salad..32

Slow Cooker Beef and Broccoli...32

Crockpot Chicken Fajita Soup...33

Slow Cooker Spicy Shrimp Soup...33

Crockpot Mediterranean Vegetable Stew..34

Slow Cooker Keto Clam Chowder...34

Crockpot Sausage and Peppers..35

DINNER...**37**

Slow Cooker Garlic Butter Chicken Thighs..38

Keto Crockpot Spaghetti Squash and Meatballs..38

Slow Cooked Beef Short Ribs in Red Wine Sauce..39

Crockpot Lemon Garlic Butter Salmon...39

Slow Cooker Creamy Tuscan Chicken...40

Crockpot Keto Jambalaya...40

Slow Cooker Balsamic Glazed Pork Tenderloin..41

Keto Crockpot Chili...41

Slow Cooker Moroccan Lamb Stew...42

Crockpot Bacon-Wrapped Chicken Breast..42

Slow Cooker Herbed Chicken and Vegetables 43

Crockpot Coconut Lime Chicken 43

Slow Cooker Spicy Beef Curry 44

Crockpot Italian Sausage and Peppers 44

Slow Cooker Lemon Pepper Turkey Breast 45

SIDE DISHES **47**

Cheesy Cauliflower Mash 48

Crockpot Garlic Parmesan Green Beans 48

Slow Cooker Spiced Brussels Sprouts 49

Keto Creamed Spinach 49

Slow Cooked Bacon and Collard Greens 50

Crockpot Herbed Almond Bread 50

Slow Cooker Garlic Herb Mushrooms 51

Crockpot Keto Cauliflower "Potato" Salad 51

Slow Cooker Cheesy Jalapeño Cornbread 52

Crockpot Creamy Ranch Cauliflower 52

Slow Cooker Cinnamon Roasted Nuts 53

Crockpot Spicy Cauliflower Rice 53

Slow Cooker Balsamic Roasted Vegetables 54

Crockpot Smoky Bacon Greens 54

Slow Cooker Lemon Asparagus 55

SNACKS AND SMALL BITES **57**

Crockpot Buffalo Chicken Dip 58

Slow Cooker Salted Caramel Pecan Pie 58

Keto Slow Cooker Cheddar Cheese Chips 59

Crockpot Spinach and Artichoke Dip 59

Slow Cooker Jalapeño Cheddar Egg Bites 60

Crockpot Keto Nachos 60

Slow Cooker Bacon-Wrapped Little Smokies 61

Crockpot Spicy Roasted Almonds 61

Slow Cooker Cheesy Garlic Breadsticks 62

Crockpot Low-Carb Meatballs 62

Slow Cooker Stuffed Jalapeños 63

Crockpot BBQ Chicken Wings 63

Slow Cooker Parmesan Ranch Mushrooms 64

Crockpot Garlic Butter Shrimp 64

Slow Cooker Smoked Paprika Almonds 65

SEAFOOD **67**

Slow Cooker Lemon Herb Salmon 68

Keto Crockpot Shrimp Scampi 68

Slow Cooker Coconut Curry Shrimp 69

Crockpot Garlic Butter Lobster Tails 69

Slow Cooker Spicy Tuna Melt Pie 70

Crockpot Seafood Chowder 70

Slow Cooker Cajun Shrimp and Sausage 71

Crockpot Lemon Dill Cod 71

Slow Cooker Spicy Crab Dip 72

Crockpot Salmon with Creamy Herb Sauce 72

Slow Cooker Garlic Parmesan Shrimp 73

CROCKPOT CLAM AND VEGETABLE MEDLEY 73

SLOW COOKER TERIYAKI SALMON AND VEGETABLES 74

CROCKPOT TOMATO BASIL SCALLOPS 74

SLOW COOKER SPICY SHRIMP JAMBALAYA 75

POULTRY 77

SLOW COOKER CHICKEN ALFREDO 78

CROCKPOT BUFFALO WINGS...78

KETO SLOW COOKER CHICKEN MARSALA 79

SLOW COOKER TURKEY AND AVOCADO CHILI 79

CROCKPOT CHICKEN PARMESAN 80

SLOW COOKER MOROCCAN CHICKEN 80

CROCKPOT SALSA VERDE CHICKEN 81

SLOW COOKER CHICKEN CACCIATORE 81

CROCKPOT BBQ CHICKEN THIGHS 82

SLOW COOKER LEMON HERB ROAST CHICKEN 82

CROCKPOT CHICKEN AND MUSHROOM GRAVY 83

SLOW COOKER TERIYAKI CHICKEN 83

CROCKPOT SPINACH AND FETA CHICKEN 84

SLOW COOKER CHICKEN TIKKA MASALA 84

CROCKPOT GREEK LEMON CHICKEN SOUP 85

MEAT 87

SLOW COOKER KETO BEEF STROGANOFF 88

CROCKPOT PULLED PORK WITH KETO BBQ SAUCE 88

SLOW COOKER LAMB CURRY 89

KETO MEATBALL SUB CASSEROLE IN A CROCKPOT 89

SLOW COOKER BACON-WRAPPED PORK LOIN 90

CROCKPOT BEEF BOURGUIGNON 90

SLOW COOKER PORK CHOPS AND GRAVY 91

CROCKPOT ITALIAN BEEF ROAST 91

SLOW COOKER SMOKY BEEF BRISKET 92

CROCKPOT CORNED BEEF AND CABBAGE...92

SLOW COOKER KOREAN BEEF SHORT RIBS 93

CROCKPOT SPICY PULLED BEEF 93

SLOW COOKER TEXAS CHILI 94

CROCKPOT MAPLE MUSTARD PORK TENDERLOIN 94

SLOW COOKER ROPA VIEJA 95

VEGETARIAN DISHES 97

SLOW COOKER CREAMY MUSHROOM STROGANOFF 98

CROCKPOT KETO VEGETABLE CURRY 98

SLOW COOKER CHEESY CAULIFLOWER CASSEROLE 99

CROCKPOT SPINACH AND FETA QUICHE 99

SLOW COOKER AVOCADO TEX-MEX SOUP 100

CROCKPOT BUTTERNUT SQUASH SOUP 100

SLOW COOKER EGGPLANT PARMESAN 101

CROCKPOT ZUCCHINI AND YELLOW SQUASH CASSEROLE 101

SLOW COOKER TOMATO AND EGGPLANT STEW 102

CROCKPOT CHEESY ASPARAGUS 102

SLOW COOKER CREAMY PUMPKIN SOUP 103

CROCKPOT LOW-CARB RATATOUILLE 103

SLOW COOKER SPICY BLACK BEAN SOUP...104

CROCKPOT GOLDEN CAULIFLOWER SOUP..104

SLOW COOKER VEGETARIAN STUFFED PEPPERS...105

DESSERTS...107

SLOW COOKER LOW-CARB CHOCOLATE LAVA CAKE...108

CROCKPOT PUMPKIN CHEESECAKE..108

KETO SLOW COOKER BERRY COBBLER..109

SLOW COOKER CINNAMON PECAN CUSTARD..109

CROCKPOT COCONUT CHOCOLATE FUDGE..110

SLOW COOKER LEMON CHEESECAKE...110

CROCKPOT SPICED APPLE CRUMBLE..111

SLOW COOKER CHOCOLATE PEANUT BUTTER CAKE...111

CROCKPOT VANILLA RICOTTA DESSERT...112

SLOW COOKER BERRY COMPOTE WITH WHIPPED CREAM..112

CROCKPOT KETO CHOCOLATE CHIP COOKIE BARS...113

SLOW COOKER ALMOND JOY CAKE...113

SLOW COOKER PEACH COBBLER..114

SLOW COOKER KETO CHOCOLATE PEANUT BUTTER PUDDING......................................114

CROCKPOT CINNAMON ROLL CASSEROLE...115

MEASUREMENT CONVERSION CHARTS...116

Mastering the Keto Diet

The ketogenic diet, commonly known as the keto diet, has gained popularity for its effectiveness in weight loss and other health benefits. It revolves around the principles of low carbohydrate intake, moderate protein consumption, and a high intake of healthy fats. To help you navigate the world of keto, we've compiled a comprehensive guide with practical tips for success.

Embarking on the keto journey requires more than just enthusiasm; it demands a solid understanding of the fundamental principles that govern this dietary approach. By taking the time to educate yourself, you lay the groundwork for a successful and sustainable experience on the ketogenic diet. Understanding the macronutrient composition of foods is paramount. In the world of keto, the focus shifts from the conventional dietary pyramid to a breakdown based on macronutrients: carbohydrates, proteins, and fats. Carbohydrates are the primary source of energy for the body. On the keto diet, the aim is to drastically reduce carbohydrate intake to induce a state of ketosis. This metabolic state prompts the body to burn fat for fuel instead of relying on glucose derived from carbs. Be diligent in identifying and limiting high-carb foods such as grains, fruits, and starchy vegetables. Proteins play a crucial role in muscle maintenance and overall bodily functions. However, excessive protein intake can potentially hinder ketosis, as the body can convert excess protein into glucose. Opt for moderate and high-quality protein sources like lean meats, fish, eggs, and dairy while being mindful of your overall intake. Contrary to conventional dietary advice, the keto diet emphasizes a high intake of healthy fats. These fats serve as the primary energy source during ketosis. Incorporate sources such as avocados, olive oil, coconut oil, nuts, and seeds. Understanding the distinction between healthy and unhealthy fats is vital for crafting a well-rounded and nutritious keto diet. Distinguishing between low-carb and high-fat options is the key to shaping your meals in alignment with the keto principles. While many whole foods naturally fit into the keto framework, it's essential to be aware of hidden sugars and processed additives that might sneak into seemingly innocent products.

Strategic planning is the linchpin of success in navigating the ketogenic diet. Cultivating a ritual of meal preparation, allocate dedicated time weekly to plan and create meals, steering clear of convenience pitfalls. A meticulously crafted keto-friendly grocery list, encompassing a variety of meats, fish, eggs, nuts, seeds, vegetables, and healthy oils, serves as your compass during shopping trips. Embrace diversity in your culinary repertoire, experimenting with flavors to sustain interest and nutrient intake. Batch cooking emerges as a time-saving ally, ensuring a ready supply of keto-approved meals. Anticipate cravings with smart snacks, maintaining flexibility when life throws curveballs. In essence, your proactive planning approach transforms potential challenges into manageable steps, fostering dietary consistency and unlocking the transformative benefits of the ketogenic lifestyle.

Hydration stands as a cornerstone in the realm of the ketogenic diet, where the body's shift into ketosis often leads to increased water loss. Recognizing this, prioritizing proper hydration becomes paramount for both well-being and sustained ketosis. The recommendation is clear: make a conscious effort to drink ample water throughout the day. This not only replenishes the fluids the body expels during the metabolic processes of ketosis but also bolsters overall health. Beyond the immediate benefits of supporting bodily functions, maintaining adequate hydration aids in mitigating potential side effects associated with transitioning into the ketogenic state. In essence, consider water as your steadfast ally, ensuring a well-hydrated foundation for your successful and health-conscious journey through the keto lifestyle.

In the intricate tapestry of a balanced diet, vegetables emerge as indispensable, playing a pivotal role in the ketogenic journey. Within the realm of the keto diet, directing your focus towards non-starchy options becomes key. Embrace the verdant goodness of leafy greens, the cruciferous delights of broccoli and cauliflower, and the vibrant hues of bell peppers. These choices not only offer a palette of essential nutrients but also contribute valuable dietary fiber without tipping the scale on carb intake. Nourishing the body with these low-carb, nutrient-dense vegetables not only enhances overall health but also aligns seamlessly with the keto philosophy. In essence, let your plate be a canvas adorned with the vibrant colors and nourishing essence of non-starchy vegetables, weaving a tapestry of both culinary delight and nutritional wisdom on your ketogenic journey.

Precision is paramount in the realm of the ketogenic diet, and vigilant tracking of your daily macronutrient intake serves as the compass guiding you towards ketosis. The delicate balance between carbohydrates, fats, and proteins requires meticulous attention, making it crucial to monitor these elements closely. In the digital age, leveraging the power of technology becomes your ally in this journey. Utilize specialized apps or online tools designed for macronutrient tracking, seamlessly integrating them into your routine. These tools not only provide real-time insights into your dietary composition but also empower you to make informed decisions, ensuring that you stay on the prescribed keto path. As you navigate this data-driven approach, remember that precision in tracking is not just a practice; it's a potent tool propelling you towards the metabolic state of ketosis, where your body optimally burns fat for energy.

In the mosaic of the ketogenic lifestyle, the embrace of healthy fats stands as a cornerstone, ushering in not only a rich tapestry of flavors but also a myriad of health benefits. Avocados, with their creamy texture, and oils such as olive oil and coconut oil become your culinary allies, adding depth and nourishment to your meals. Nuts, with their satisfying crunch, further enrich the symphony of flavors. Beyond the sensory delights, these healthy fats play a dual role, imparting a profound sense of satiety while delivering essential nutrients crucial for overall well-being. The omega-3 fatty acids in these sources not only contribute to cardiovascular health but also support cognitive function. As you navigate the world of healthy fats on the ketogenic stage, consider them not just as ingredients but as vital contributors to the holistic well-being that defines the essence of the keto lifestyle.

In sculpting your ketogenic plate, the careful selection of protein sources emerges as a crucial art form, influencing not only the flavor profile but also the integrity of your keto journey. Opt for high-quality, lean proteins, such as the versatility of poultry, the omega-3 richness of fish, the nutrient density of eggs, and the ethical choice of grass-fed meat. These selections not only fuel your body with essential amino acids but also align seamlessly with the keto philosophy. As you curate your protein choices, navigate away from the pitfalls of processed and cured meats, where hidden sugars may disrupt the purity of your keto diet. Let the purity of your protein sources mirror the clarity of your commitment to the ketogenic lifestyle, where quality and conscious choices intertwine to shape a plate that not only delights the palate but also honors the essence of optimal health.

Navigating the waters of the ketogenic diet involves not only a mindful consideration of macronutrients but also a keen awareness of electrolyte balance. The shift into ketosis can influence the body's sodium, potassium, and magnesium levels, making it imperative to be proactive in maintaining these essential electrolytes. To safeguard against symptoms such as muscle cramps or fatigue, prioritize foods rich in these minerals. Incorporate sodium through sources like salt, potassium through foods like avocados and leafy greens, and magnesium through nuts and seeds. Additionally, considering electrolyte supplements can be beneficial, especially if you find it challenging to meet these requirements solely through food.

By taking a deliberate approach to electrolyte balance, you not only enhance your well-being on the ketogenic journey but also foster a smoother transition into the metabolic state of ketosis.

In the realm of the ketogenic lifestyle, consistency stands tall as an unwavering pillar of success. Adhering steadfastly to the prescribed macronutrient ratios is the linchpin that sustains the metabolic state of ketosis. The delicate balance of low carbohydrates, moderate proteins, and high-quality fats is not a mere guideline but a blueprint for achieving and maintaining optimal results. The essence of keto success lies in the commitment to this framework, resisting the allure of frequent deviations that could disrupt the delicate balance. It is this unwavering commitment, this day-in and day-out consistency, that propels you toward the myriad benefits of the ketogenic state, making it not just a diet but a steadfast journey towards transformative well-being.

Embarking on a ketogenic lifestyle is a transformative journey that unfolds gradually, and patience becomes a valuable ally in this process of adaptation. Anticipate and embrace the initial challenges, often referred to as the "keto flu," which might manifest as headaches and fatigue. These symptoms, while temporary, signify your body's adjustment to a new metabolic paradigm. It's crucial to recognize that this transitional phase is a natural part of the journey, akin to your body recalibrating its energy sources. As you persist with the ketogenic lifestyle, rest assured that these initial hurdles typically subside over time. Your body's resilience and adaptability come to the forefront, and the discomfort gradually transforms into a renewed sense of energy and well-being, marking the evolution into a state of sustained ketosis. Embrace the journey with resilience, knowing that the initial challenges are stepping stones toward the lasting benefits of a ketogenic lifestyle.

Prior to undertaking any dietary endeavor, especially one as specific as the ketogenic diet, it is paramount to seek guidance from healthcare professionals or registered dietitians. These experts possess the knowledge to offer personalized advice, taking into account your unique health status, medical history, and individual goals. Consulting with a healthcare professional ensures that you embark on the keto journey safely, mitigating potential risks and aligning the dietary approach with your overall well-being. Their insights can encompass considerations such as pre-existing medical conditions, medication interactions, and any specific nutritional needs you may have. By initiating this dialogue with a healthcare professional or registered dietitian, you not only fortify your keto experience with informed decisions but also prioritize your health in a holistic and sustainable manner.

In conclusion, the ketogenic diet presents a distinctive avenue for weight management and holistic well-being. By embracing the tips provided and adhering to a well-balanced, nutrient-rich diet, you set the stage for a successful keto journey that aligns seamlessly with your health and wellness aspirations. It is crucial to stay informed, allowing knowledge to be your guide as you navigate this transformative dietary approach. Patience becomes a virtue in adapting to the nuances of the keto lifestyle, recognizing that enduring benefits often arise with steadfast commitment. Importantly, seeking professional guidance, be it from healthcare professionals or registered dietitians, ensures that your keto experience is not only effective but also sustainable in the long run. As you embark on this unique dietary path, remember that the keys to success lie in a combination of knowledge, perseverance, and a commitment to your individual health goals.

What to Eat and Avoid for Success

The ketogenic diet has gained popularity for its effective approach to weight management and overall health. Central to its success is a meticulous selection of foods to eat and a deliberate avoidance of certain items. In this article, we'll explore the essentials of what to include and what to steer clear of to make the most of your keto journey.

What to Eat on a Keto Diet?

Embracing a variety of healthy fats serves as the cornerstone of fueling your ketogenic journey with vitality and nutritional richness. Avocados, with their creamy texture and abundance of monounsaturated fats, become a versatile addition, contributing not only to the diet's fat content but also supplying essential nutrients like potassium and fiber. The inclusion of olive oil introduces heart-healthy monounsaturated fats and antioxidants, offering both flavor enhancement and nutritional benefits. Coconut oil, renowned for its medium-chain triglycerides, becomes a potent energy source, fostering ketone production. Nuts and seeds, such as almonds, walnuts, chia seeds, and flaxseeds, bring a satisfying crunch to meals while delivering a bounty of omega-3 fatty acids, fiber, and essential minerals. This symphony of healthy fats not only satiates the palate but also ensures that your body thrives on the diverse array of nutrients, providing sustained energy and supporting overall well-being throughout your ketogenic journey.

Choosing lean, high-quality proteins is a pivotal aspect of mastering the ketogenic lifestyle, striking a delicate balance between fulfilling protein needs and minimizing carb intake. Poultry, such as chicken and turkey, takes center stage as a lean protein source that aligns seamlessly with the principles of the keto diet. Fish, with its omega-3 fatty acids, not only supports cardiovascular health but also provides a high-quality protein option. Eggs, a nutritional powerhouse, offer a versatile and affordable protein source, enriched with essential amino acids. Opting for grass-fed meat introduces a higher concentration of omega-3s and ensures a cleaner protein profile. By prioritizing these protein sources, you not only support muscle health and satiety but also lay the foundation for a ketogenic journey where nutritional quality complements macronutrient composition, fostering a holistic approach to overall well-being.

Non-starchy vegetables stand as nutritional powerhouses in the realm of the ketogenic diet, contributing both vibrancy and essential nutrients to your meals. Leafy greens, like spinach and kale, emerge as low-carb, high-fiber champions, packed with vitamins, minerals, and antioxidants. Broccoli and cauliflower, versatile cruciferous vegetables, not only provide fiber but also offer a host of vitamins and compounds with potential health benefits. Bell peppers, with their spectrum of colors, bring not just visual appeal but also a generous dose of vitamin C and other antioxidants. These non-starchy vegetables become the canvas upon which you craft nutrient-dense, flavorful dishes, ensuring that your ketogenic journey is not only health-conscious but also a vibrant culinary adventure.

Indulging in full-fat dairy products becomes a delightful and nutritious component of your ketogenic repertoire, offering both flavor and essential healthy fats. Cheese, with its diverse textures and flavors, emerges as a savory ally, providing a rich source of saturated fats and protein. Butter, a culinary classic, not only enhances the taste of your dishes but also contributes to the high-fat requirements of the keto diet. However, maintaining awareness of carbohydrate content is key, as some dairy products may contain hidden sugars or carbs. By savoring full-fat dairy judiciously, you not only elevate the palatability of your meals but also ensure a mindful balance within the carbohydrate constraints of the ketogenic lifestyle.

Elevating your ketogenic experience with a satisfying crunch and a wealth of nutritional benefits involves the incorporation of almonds, walnuts, chia seeds, and flaxseeds into your dietary repertoire. Almonds, with their nutrient density, offer a delightful crunch alongside a rich source of healthy fats, fiber, and vitamin E. Walnuts, shaped like miniature brains, provide omega-3 fatty acids and antioxidants, contributing to heart health and overall well-being. Chia seeds, tiny powerhouses, expand when soaked, creating a satisfying texture while delivering a dose of omega-3s, fiber, and essential minerals. Flaxseeds, with their nutty flavor, add not only a pleasant crunch but also a wealth of omega-3 fatty acids and lignans. By incorporating this quartet of crunchy goodness, you not only infuse variety into your meals but also fortify your body with a nutrient-rich ensemble, aligning seamlessly with the principles of the ketogenic lifestyle.

Embarking on the ketogenic journey with fish and seafood, particularly the fatty varieties like salmon and mackerel, unveils a treasure trove of nutritional benefits. These aquatic marvels not only tantalize the taste buds but also deliver a robust source of omega-3 fatty acids, promoting heart health, reducing inflammation, and supporting cognitive function. Beyond their omega-3 prowess, fish and seafood present a high-quality protein source, essential for muscle maintenance and overall bodily functions. The inclusion of these marine delicacies not only adds diversity to your meals but also fortifies your ketogenic experience with a symphony of flavors and nutrients, aligning seamlessly with the diet's principles of optimal health and well-being.

Eggs stand as a quintessential cornerstone in the realm of the ketogenic diet, offering versatility, nutrition, and culinary delight. This humble yet mighty ingredient presents itself as a keto-friendly powerhouse, providing essential amino acids, high-quality protein, and healthy fats. Whether enjoyed scrambled, poached, or as part of a satisfying omelet, eggs become a canvas upon which you can craft a variety of keto-friendly breakfasts and meals. Their nutritional profile not only supports muscle maintenance and overall bodily functions but also aligns seamlessly with the macronutrient composition essential for sustaining ketosis. In the world of ketogenic living, eggs emerge as a dependable and delightful ally, contributing not only to the nutritional richness of your meals but also to the culinary diversity that makes your keto journey both wholesome and enjoyable.

Navigating the world of sweetness on a ketogenic diet involves the strategic use of sugar substitutes, with stevia and erythritol emerging as star players. These sugar alternatives offer a welcome touch of sweetness to your dishes without causing spikes in carbohydrate intake. Stevia, derived from the leaves of the Stevia rebaudiana plant, provides a natural sweetness without impacting blood sugar levels. Erythritol, a sugar alcohol, adds sweetness without the caloric or glycemic load associated with traditional sugars. By incorporating these sugar substitutes, you can indulge your sweet tooth without veering off the keto path. Be mindful, however, of individual preferences and reactions to sugar substitutes, and enjoy these alternatives in moderation to maintain the integrity of your low-carb lifestyle.

Elevating your culinary creations on the ketogenic journey involves embracing the vibrant world of herbs and spices, where flavor takes center stage without compromising your commitment to low-carb living. Herbs like basil, cilantro, and thyme infuse freshness, while spices such as cumin, paprika, and turmeric bring depth and complexity. This aromatic symphony not only enhances the taste of your meals but also elevates the overall dining experience without introducing unnecessary carbohydrates. The versatility of herbs and spices empowers you to craft diverse and delicious dishes, ensuring that your ketogenic lifestyle is not only health-conscious but a celebration of rich and satisfying flavors. So, let your kitchen become a playground of aromatic delights, where herbs and spices become the culinary maestros guiding your palate through a symphony of keto-friendly sensations.

What to Avoid on a Keto Diet?

Navigating the ketogenic path requires a conscious effort to steer clear of high-carb culprits that could derail your progress. Bid farewell to grains, where wheat, barley, and oats take a back seat, making way for a carb-conscious approach. Bread, pasta, and rice, staples in many diets, find alternative paths as you stay within the defined limits of keto carbohydrates. Fruits, though nature's sweet bounty, beckon caution, with choices like bananas, grapes, and mangoes being approached sparingly due to their higher sugar content. By sidestepping these high-carb contenders, you not only honor the principles of the ketogenic lifestyle but also pave the way for sustained ketosis and the myriad benefits it brings to your health and well-being.

In the pursuit of ketosis, a fundamental rule is to eliminate sugary temptations that could potentially derail your efforts. Bid farewell to the allure of candy, cookies, cakes, and sweetened drinks, as these sugary delights not only contribute to excess carbohydrate intake but also pose a threat to the metabolic state of ketosis. By steering clear of these sugary indulgences, you safeguard the delicate balance required for the ketogenic lifestyle. Instead, opt for satisfying alternatives that align with your low-carb goals, allowing you to indulge in the sweet taste of success while staying true to the principles of a carb-conscious and health-conscious ketogenic journey.

In the realm of the ketogenic diet, a strategic move involves minimizing the presence of starchy vegetables like potatoes, corn, and carrots in your culinary repertoire. While these vegetables offer nutritional benefits, their higher carbohydrate content can act as a potential impediment to achieving and maintaining ketosis. By being mindful of your intake of starchy vegetables, you ensure that your carbohydrate allowance is dedicated to nutrient-dense, low-carb options, thus promoting the metabolic state essential for the success of the ketogenic lifestyle. In this calculated approach, you not only prioritize your low-carb goals but also optimize your journey toward the transformative benefits that ketosis brings to your health and well-being.

Embracing the principles of the ketogenic diet involves a resolute stance against highly processed foods, recognizing them as potential adversaries in your journey towards nutritional well-being. These processed culprits often harbor hidden sugars and unhealthy fats that can disrupt the delicate balance required for successful ketosis. By saying no to these convenient yet nutritionally dubious options, you not only shield yourself from hidden pitfalls but also reinforce the purity of your dietary choices. Opt for whole, unprocessed foods to ensure that your body receives the essential nutrients it needs without compromising your commitment to a low-carb and health-conscious ketogenic lifestyle.

When navigating the world of sauces and condiments on a ketogenic journey, a crucial strategy is to diligently check labels for added sugars. Many commercial sauces and condiments can sneak in hidden carbs, potentially hindering your progress in maintaining ketosis. Opt for a discerning approach, choosing homemade versions or sugar-free alternatives that align with your low-carb goals. By making this conscious choice, you not only infuse your meals with flavor without compromising on carb counts but also maintain the integrity of your ketogenic lifestyle. This vigilant label scrutiny ensures that each condiment contributes to your culinary experience without introducing unnecessary carbohydrates, empowering you to savor the richness of flavor while staying true to your health-conscious objectives.

In the realm of the ketogenic lifestyle, a crucial tactic for maintaining low-carb integrity is meticulous label scrutiny, particularly when it comes to sauces and condiments. Commercial varieties often harbor added sugars, which can unwittingly tip the scales on your carb intake.

A prudent strategy involves opting for a homemade approach or selecting sugar-free alternatives to ensure that these flavor enhancers align seamlessly with your ketogenic goals. By exercising this discerning choice, you not only curate a palate-pleasing experience but also safeguard your commitment to a low-carb existence. This mindful consideration of labels becomes a key tool in your arsenal, allowing you to savor the diverse flavors of your meals while avoiding unnecessary carbohydrates and staying true to the essence of the ketogenic lifestyle.

In the pursuit of ketosis, a judicious approach to fruit consumption becomes paramount, especially when dealing with high-sugar fruits such as bananas, grapes, and mangoes. While these fruits offer natural sweetness and nutritional benefits, their elevated sugar content can lead to an excess of carbohydrates, potentially hindering your ketogenic goals. Therefore, it's prudent to limit the intake of these particular fruits, opting instead for lower-sugar alternatives like berries or avocados, which align more closely with the carbohydrate restrictions of the ketogenic diet. By exercising this moderation, you ensure that your fruit choices contribute to your overall health without compromising the delicate balance required for sustained ketosis.

Steering clear of trans fats is a wise and health-conscious decision, especially when navigating the realm of processed and fried foods. Trans fats, commonly found in these culinary offerings, can exert adverse effects on your health, contributing to elevated levels of bad cholesterol and an increased risk of cardiovascular issues. By avoiding these unhealthy fats, you safeguard your well-being and align with the principles of the ketogenic lifestyle, which prioritizes nutrient-dense, whole foods. Opt for cooking methods that utilize healthier fats, such as olive oil or coconut oil, and choose minimally processed alternatives to ensure that your dietary choices contribute positively to both your ketogenic goals and overall health.

In the context of a ketogenic lifestyle, exercising moderation or even considering the elimination of alcohol consumption is a prudent choice. Alcohol can interfere with the state of ketosis, disrupting the metabolic process and potentially slowing down progress. Moreover, alcoholic beverages often contribute empty calories without providing essential nutrients, posing a challenge to the carb-conscious and health-conscious objectives of the ketogenic diet. By exercising caution with alcohol intake, you not only support your commitment to maintaining ketosis but also optimize your dietary choices for overall well-being. Choosing alternatives such as water, herbal teas, or low-carb options aligns more harmoniously with the principles of the ketogenic lifestyle, allowing you to savor the benefits without compromising your health-conscious goals.

When navigating the dairy aisle on your ketogenic journey, a strategic choice is to opt for full-fat dairy products over their low-fat or fat-free counterparts. While the latter may seem like healthier options, they often come with hidden pitfalls in the form of added sugars. Full-fat dairy, on the other hand, provides a source of healthy fats without the unwanted sugars that can interfere with your ketogenic efforts. This conscious choice not only supports the macronutrient balance essential for ketosis but also ensures that you are making nutritionally sound decisions in alignment with the principles of the ketogenic lifestyle. By prioritizing full-fat dairy, you create a pathway for sustained ketosis while enjoying the rich and satisfying flavors these products offer.

In adhering to the principles of the ketogenic diet, it's crucial to navigate away from grains such as wheat, barley, and oats. These grain staples, while dietary mainstays in conventional nutrition, are notably high in carbohydrates, making them incompatible with the low-carb ethos of the keto lifestyle.

By steering clear of these high-carb grains, you not only uphold the foundational principles of ketosis but also optimize your carbohydrate intake for sustained metabolic benefits. Embrace alternatives like almond flour, coconut flour, or flaxseed meal to craft keto-friendly versions of your favorite baked goods, allowing you to relish the flavors while staying true to the essence of the ketogenic diet.

Successfully navigating the keto lifestyle involves a thoughtful selection of foods that align with the diet's principles. By incorporating healthy fats, lean proteins, low-carb vegetables, and mindful choices, you set the stage for a successful ketogenic journey. Conversely, avoiding high-carb and processed foods is equally crucial to maintain the metabolic state of ketosis. As you embark on your keto adventure, remember that individual responses may vary, and consulting with healthcare professionals or registered dietitians can provide personalized guidance for a safe and effective experience. With these guidelines in mind, you're equipped to embark on a keto journey that harmonizes with your health and wellness goals.

Tips for Effective Slow Cooking

Going deeper into the idea of this book serving as a guide for slow cooker recipes, let's delve into additional insights to boost the success of your culinary journey. These tips are designed to streamline your cooking process and enhance the flavors and textures of your dishes. Whether you're an experienced slow cooker enthusiast or a beginner, integrating these suggestions can contribute to a more enjoyable and satisfying cooking experience.

When choosing a slow cooker, consider your specific needs. Opt for a larger size if you plan on batch cooking or preparing meals for the whole family. This is especially convenient for hearty stews or large cuts of meat. Conversely, if you're cooking for smaller portions or experimenting with new recipes, a smaller slow cooker is more suitable. Customizing the size to your intended use ensures optimal results and makes your slow cooking experience more efficient and enjoyable.

Efficiency is crucial in slow cooking, and preparing ingredients the night before can significantly streamline your mornings. Take the time in the evening to chop vegetables, marinate meats, or measure out spices. This foresight allows you to assemble your meal quickly in the morning, minimizing the rush and making the start of your slow cooking process smooth and stress-free. This simple yet effective tip not only saves time but also ensures that you can savor a delicious, well-prepared meal with minimal morning hassle.

Achieving even cooking in your slow cooker is an art, and strategic layering plays a crucial role. Place meats at the bottom of the slow cooker and delicate vegetables on top to ensure optimal results. This method allows the meat to absorb flavors from the ingredients below while preventing the vegetables from becoming overly mushy during the extended cooking process. By mastering the art of ingredient layering, you enhance the overall taste and texture of your slow-cooked dishes.

In the realm of slow cooking, managing liquid levels is pivotal. Unlike traditional cooking methods, slow cookers require less liquid. When adapting a recipe from stovetop or oven cooking to the slow cooker, it's essential to reduce the amount of liquid used. This adjustment ensures that your slow-cooked dishes achieve the desired consistency and intensity of flavors. By being mindful of liquid levels, you not only embrace the unique dynamics of slow cooking but also guarantee that your creations are perfectly balanced and rich in taste, making the most out of every ingredient.

Maintaining a closed lid is a cardinal rule in slow cooking. Every time you lift the lid, valuable heat escapes, and this can substantially extend the cooking time. Resist the temptation to peek unnecessarily. Only open the lid when essential tasks like stirring or adding ingredients midway are required. This discipline preserves the consistent heat and ensures that your slow cooker functions optimally, resulting in perfectly cooked and flavorful dishes. By embracing this patience-driven approach, you contribute to the success of your slow-cooked creations, achieving the desired tenderness and melding of flavors without unnecessary disruptions.

Precision in temperature is a key factor in successful slow cooking. Adhere to the temperature guidelines specified in your recipe. Opting for the low setting and allowing for a more extended cooking period often leads to tender and more flavorful results. This gentle, prolonged cooking process allows flavors to meld, and tougher cuts of meat to become succulent. By respecting the suggested temperature settings, you harness the full potential of your slow cooker, ensuring that each dish reaches its peak of tenderness and taste.

When incorporating dairy into your slow-cooked dishes, timing is crucial to avoid unwanted curdling. Milk or cream should be stirred in during the last 15-30 minutes of the cooking process. Adding dairy too early can lead to curdling due to the prolonged exposure to heat. By introducing dairy towards the end, you preserve its creamy texture and enhance the overall richness of your dish. This careful timing ensures that your slow-cooked creations maintain a smooth and luscious consistency, delivering a delightful and well-balanced culinary experience.

Elevate the freshness and aroma of your slow-cooked dishes by incorporating fresh herbs towards the end of the cooking time. Their delicate flavors are best preserved when added closer to completion. On the other hand, dried herbs can be introduced earlier in the process, allowing their robust notes to infuse gradually. This thoughtful approach ensures that the essence of fresh herbs enhances your dish, providing a burst of flavor right before serving. By mastering the timing of herb additions, you infuse your slow-cooked meals with a harmonious blend of fragrances that captivate the palate.

Achieving the perfect consistency is key in slow cooking. If your dish is too watery, employ strategic methods to enhance thickness. Firstly, uncover the slow cooker for the last 30 minutes of cooking to allow some moisture to evaporate and the sauce to naturally thicken. Alternatively, for more immediate results, consider creating a slurry by mixing cornstarch with water. Stir this slurry into your dish, and the sauce will thicken as it continues to simmer. This versatile technique empowers you to fine-tune the texture of your slow-cooked creations, ensuring a satisfying and well-balanced culinary experience.

Simplify your post-cooking routine by adopting a proactive approach to cleanup. Consider using slow cooker liners or spraying the interior with non-stick cooking spray before adding ingredients. Slow cooker liners provide a convenient barrier that makes cleanup a breeze, while a light coating of non-stick spray minimizes the chances of ingredients sticking to the surface. Embracing these easy cleanup practices ensures that the joy of slow cooking extends beyond the kitchen, allowing you to savor your delicious creations without the hassle of extensive scrubbing afterward.

By adhering to the advice provided above, you can optimize your cooking experience with a slow cooker. From selecting the right size to strategic ingredient preparation and managing liquid levels, these tips cover various aspects to ensure that your slow-cooked dishes are not only delicious but also prepared with efficiency and ease. Incorporating these practices will enhance your overall enjoyment of slow cooker cooking, making it a rewarding and convenient culinary experience.

Breakfast

Keto Slow Cooker Spinach and Feta Frittata

INGREDIENTS

- 8 large eggs
- 1 cup heavy cream
- 2 cups fresh spinach, chopped
- 1 cup feta cheese, crumbled
- 1/2 cup diced red bell pepper
- 1/4 cup diced onion
- 1 teaspoon salt
- 1/2 teaspoon black pepper
- 1/2 teaspoon garlic powder
- Butter or olive oil for greasing

 Prep Time: 10 min   Cook Time: 2 hours   Serves: 4

DIRECTIONS

In a large bowl, whisk together the eggs, heavy cream, salt, black pepper, and garlic powder until well combined. Grease the slow cooker insert with butter or olive oil. Add the chopped spinach, diced red bell pepper, and diced onion to the slow cooker. Pour the egg mixture over the vegetables in the slow cooker. Sprinkle the crumbled feta cheese on top. Cover and cook on low for 2 hours, or until the eggs are set and the frittata is cooked through.

NUTRITIONAL INFORMATION

Per serving: 400 calories, 24g protein, 6g carbohydrates, 32g fat, 1g fiber, 440mg cholesterol, 980mg sodium, 350mg potassium.

Low-Carb Blueberry Lemon Breakfast Cake

INGREDIENTS

- 2 cups almond flour
- 1/2 cup coconut flour
- 1/4 cup erythritol (or other keto-friendly sweetener)
- 1 teaspoon baking powder
- 1/2 teaspoon salt
- Zest of 1 lemon
- 4 large eggs
- 1/2 cup unsweetened almond milk
- 1/4 cup melted coconut oil
- 1 teaspoon vanilla extract
- 1 cup fresh blueberries

 Prep Time: 15 min   Cook Time: 2.5 hours   Serves: 6

DIRECTIONS

In a large bowl, mix together almond flour, coconut flour, erythritol, baking powder, salt, and lemon zest. In a separate bowl, whisk the eggs, almond milk, melted coconut oil, and vanilla extract until well combined. Pour the wet ingredients into the dry ingredients and mix until just combined. Gently fold in the blueberries. Grease the slow cooker insert with coconut oil or line it with parchment paper. Pour the batter into the slow cooker. Cover and cook on low for 2.5 hours or until a toothpick inserted into the center comes out clean. Let the cake cool before serving.

NUTRITIONAL INFORMATION

Per serving: 320 calories, 12g protein, 14g carbohydrates, 26g fat, 6g fiber, 124mg cholesterol, 220mg sodium, 130mg potassium.

Slow Cooked Spicy Sausage and Egg Casserole

INGREDIENTS

- 1 pound spicy Italian sausage, casings removed
- 12 large eggs
- 1 cup heavy cream
- 1 cup shredded cheddar cheese
- 1/2 cup diced green bell pepper
- 1/2 cup diced red onion
- 1 teaspoon salt
- 1/2 teaspoon black pepper
- 1/4 teaspoon red pepper flakes (adjust to taste)
- Butter or olive oil for greasing

 Prep Time: 20 min

 Cook Time: 6 hours

 Serves: 6

DIRECTIONS

In a skillet over medium heat, cook the sausage until browned and crumbled. Drain any excess grease. In a large bowl, whisk together the eggs, heavy cream, salt, black pepper, and red pepper flakes. Stir in the cooked sausage, shredded cheese, bell pepper, and red onion. Grease the slow cooker insert with butter or olive oil. Pour the egg mixture into the slow cooker. Cover and cook on low for 6 hours, or until the eggs are set and the casserole is cooked through. Serve warm.

NUTRITIONAL INFORMATION

Per serving: 450 calories, 28g protein, 5g carbohydrates, 36g fat, 0g fiber, 390mg cholesterol, 870mg sodium, 300mg potassium.

Crockpot Pumpkin Spice Latte Oatmeal

INGREDIENTS

- 1 cup hemp hearts
- 1 cup almond flour
- 2 cups unsweetened almond milk
- 1 cup pumpkin puree
- 1/4 cup erythritol (or another keto-friendly sweetener)
- 2 teaspoons pumpkin pie spice
- 1 teaspoon vanilla extract
- 1/2 cup brewed espresso or strong coffee
- 1/4 teaspoon salt

 Prep Time: 10 minutes

 Cook Time: 6 hours

 Serves: 4

DIRECTIONS

In the crockpot, combine hemp hearts, almond flour, almond milk, pumpkin puree, erythritol, pumpkin pie spice, vanilla extract, espresso, and salt. Stir well to ensure the mixture is evenly combined. Cover and set the crockpot to low. Cook for 6 hours, stirring occasionally if possible, to prevent sticking and ensure even cooking. Once cooked, give the "oatmeal" a good stir. If the mixture is too thick, you can adjust the consistency by adding a little more almond milk until your desired texture is achieved. Serve warm with a dollop of whipped cream and a sprinkle of cinnamon or pumpkin pie spice on top, if desired.

NUTRITIONAL INFORMATION

Per serving: 350 calories, 14g protein, 12g carbohydrates, 27g fat, 6g fiber, 0mg cholesterol, 200mg sodium, 300mg potassium.

Bacon and Mushroom Keto Quiche

INGREDIENTS

- 6 large eggs
- 1 cup heavy cream
- 1 cup shredded Swiss cheese
- 1/2 pound bacon, cooked and crumbled
- 1 cup mushrooms, sliced
- 1/4 cup green onions, chopped
- 1 teaspoon salt
- 1/2 teaspoon black pepper
- Butter for greasing

 Prep Time: 15 minutes

 Cook Time: 4 hours

 Serves: 6

DIRECTIONS

In a large bowl, whisk together eggs, heavy cream, salt, and black pepper. Stir in the shredded Swiss cheese, cooked and crumbled bacon, sliced mushrooms, and green onions until well combined. Grease the inside of the slow cooker pot with butter. Pour the egg mixture into the slow cooker. Cover and cook on low for 4 hours, or until the quiche is set and the edges are slightly golden brown. Once done, let the quiche stand for a few minutes before cutting into it. Serve warm.

NUTRITIONAL INFORMATION

Per serving: 410 calories, 25g protein, 3g carbohydrates, 34g fat, 0g fiber, 345mg cholesterol, 870mg sodium, 200mg potassium.

Slow Cooker Cheesy Avocado Breakfast Casserole

INGREDIENTS

- 8 large eggs
- 1/2 cup heavy cream
- 1 ripe avocado, cubed
- 1 cup shredded cheddar cheese
- 1/2 cup cooked and crumbled bacon
- 1/4 cup diced red bell pepper
- 1/4 cup diced onion
- 1 teaspoon salt
- 1/2 teaspoon black pepper
- Non-stick cooking spray or butter for greasing

 Prep Time: 15 min

 Cook Time: 4 hours

 Serves: 4

DIRECTIONS

In a large bowl, whisk together the eggs and heavy cream until well combined. Season with salt and black pepper. Stir in the cubed avocado, shredded cheddar cheese, crumbled bacon, diced red bell pepper, and diced onion. Grease the inside of the slow cooker with non-stick cooking spray or butter. Pour the egg mixture into the slow cooker. Cover and cook on low for 4 hours, or until the casserole is set and the edges begin to lightly brown. Let the casserole cool for a few minutes before serving. Serve warm.

NUTRITIONAL INFORMATION

Per serving: 480 calories, 32g protein, 8g carbohydrates, 36g fat, 4g fiber, 425mg cholesterol, 960mg sodium, 500mg potassium.

Crockpot Cinnamon Almond Breakfast Porridge

INGREDIENTS

- 1 cup almond flour
- 1/2 cup flaxseed meal
- 2 tablespoons chia seeds
- 4 cups unsweetened almond milk
- 1/4 cup erythritol (or another keto-friendly sweetener)
- 2 teaspoons ground cinnamon
- 1 teaspoon vanilla extract
- 1/4 teaspoon salt
- Sliced almonds and additional cinnamon for topping

 Prep Time: 10 min Cook Time: 8 hours Serves: 4

DIRECTIONS

In the slow cooker, combine almond flour, flaxseed meal, chia seeds, almond milk, erythritol, ground cinnamon, vanilla extract, and salt. Stir well to ensure everything is evenly mixed. Cover and set the slow cooker to low. Cook for 8 hours, ideally overnight, until the porridge is thick and creamy. Stir the porridge well in the morning before serving. Serve hot, garnished with sliced almonds and a sprinkle of cinnamon on top. For a thinner porridge, you can add more almond milk to achieve your desired consistency.

NUTRITIONAL INFORMATION

Per serving: 350 calories, 14g protein, 16g carbohydrates, 27g fat, 10g fiber, 0mg cholesterol, 240mg sodium, 400mg potassium.

Slow Cooker Sausage and Peppers Breakfast Hash

INGREDIENTS

- 1 pound Italian sausage, casings removed and crumbled
- 1 large bell pepper, diced (color of your choice)
- 1 medium onion, diced
- 2 cloves garlic, minced
- 1 pound radishes, trimmed and quartered (as a low-carb potato substitute)
- 1 teaspoon smoked paprika
- 1/2 teaspoon salt
- 1/4 teaspoon black pepper
- 4 large eggs (optional, to be added in the last 30 minutes of cooking)
- Fresh parsley for garnish

 Prep Time: 15 min  Cook Time: 6 hours Serves: 4

DIRECTIONS

In a skillet over medium heat, brown the sausage with the onion, garlic, and bell pepper until the sausage is fully cooked and vegetables are softened. Transfer the mixture to the slow cooker. Add the quartered radishes to the slow cooker, along with smoked paprika, salt, and black pepper. Stir well to combine. Cover and cook on low for 6 hours, until the radishes are tender. In the last 30 minutes of cooking, create four wells in the hash and crack an egg into each. Cover and continue cooking until the eggs are set to your liking.
Garnish with fresh parsley before serving.

NUTRITIONAL INFORMATION

Per serving: 480 calories, 28g protein, 8g carbohydrates, 36g fat, 3g fiber, 235mg cholesterol, 900mg sodium, 500mg potassium.

Crockpot Vanilla Bean and Berry Compote

INGREDIENTS

- 3 cups mixed berries (such as strawberries, blueberries, raspberries, and blackberries), fresh or frozen
- 1/4 cup water
- 1/4 cup erythritol or another keto-friendly sweetener
- 1 vanilla bean, split lengthwise and seeds scraped
- Zest of 1 lemon

Prep Time: 10 min

Cook Time: 2 hours

Serves: 4

DIRECTIONS

Combine the mixed berries, water, erythritol, and the seeds scraped from the vanilla bean in the slow cooker. Add the split vanilla bean pod and lemon zest for extra flavor. Cover and cook on low for 2 hours, until the berries have softened and the mixture has thickened slightly. Stir occasionally during cooking to ensure even heating. Once done, remove the vanilla bean pod and lemon zest. Use a fork or potato masher to lightly mash the berries to your desired consistency. Let the compote cool slightly before serving. It can be served warm or chilled.

NUTRITIONAL INFORMATION

Per serving: 50 calories, 1g protein, 12g carbohydrates, 0g fat, 3g fiber, 0mg cholesterol, 0mg sodium, 100mg potassium.

Slow Cooker Mexican Breakfast Casserole

INGREDIENTS

- 8 large eggs
- 1/2 cup heavy cream
- 1 lb ground chorizo (or Mexican sausage), cooked and drained
- 1 cup shredded cheddar cheese
- 1 cup diced bell peppers
- 1/2 cup diced onion
- 1 jalapeño, seeded and finely chopped
- 1 teaspoon chili powder
- 1/2 teaspoon cumin
- 1/2 teaspoon salt
- 1/4 teaspoon black pepper

Prep Time: 20 min   Cook Time: 4 hours   Serves: 6 servings

DIRECTIONS

In a skillet over medium heat, cook the chorizo until fully cooked. Drain any excess fat and set aside. In a large bowl, whisk together the eggs, heavy cream, chili powder, cumin, salt, and black pepper. Stir in the cooked chorizo, shredded cheese, diced bell peppers, diced onion, and chopped jalapeño (if using). Grease the inside of the slow cooker pot with non-stick cooking spray or butter. Pour the egg mixture into the slow cooker. Cover and cook on low for 4 hours, or until the eggs are set and the casserole is cooked through. Serve hot, garnished with avocado slices and fresh cilantro, if desired.

NUTRITIONAL INFORMATION

Per serving: 390 calories, 26g protein, 5g carbohydrates, 30g fat, 1g fiber, 345mg cholesterol, 890mg sodium, 200mg potassium.

Keto Crockpot Chorizo and Egg Scramble

INGREDIENTS

- 8 large eggs
- 1/2 cup heavy cream
- 1 lb chorizo sausage, casing removed and crumbled
- 1/2 cup shredded cheddar cheese
- 1/4 cup diced green bell pepper
- 1/4 cup diced red onion
- 1/4 teaspoon salt
- 1/4 teaspoon black pepper
- Non-stick cooking spray or butter for greasing

 Prep Time: 10 min Cook Time: 3 hours Serves: 4

DIRECTIONS

Cook crumbled chorizo in a skillet over medium heat until fully cooked (5-7 minutes). Drain excess fat and set aside. Beat eggs and heavy cream in a large bowl. Stir in cooked chorizo, shredded cheese, diced green bell pepper, and diced red onion. Season with salt and pepper. Grease slow cooker, pour in the egg mixture. Cover and cook on low for 3 hours until eggs are set. Stir gently once or twice during cooking if possible. Serve hot from the slow cooker.

NUTRITIONAL INFORMATION

Per serving: 480 calories, 32g protein, 4g carbohydrates, 38g fat, 0g fiber, 435mg cholesterol, 990mg sodium, 300mg potassium.

Crockpot Coconut Cream and Nut Granola

INGREDIENTS

- 1 cup unsweetened shredded coconut
- 1/2 cup sliced almonds
- 1/2 cup chopped pecans
- 1/4 cup sunflower seeds
- 1/4 cup pumpkin seeds
- 2 tablespoons chia seeds
- 1/4 cup coconut oil, melted
- 1/4 cup coconut cream
- 2 tablespoons erythritol (or other keto-friendly sweetener)
- 1 teaspoon vanilla extract
- 1/2 teaspoon cinnamon
- Pinch of salt

 Prep Time: 15 min Cook Time: 2 hours Serves: 4

DIRECTIONS

In a large bowl, mix together the shredded coconut, sliced almonds, chopped pecans, sunflower seeds, pumpkin seeds, and chia seeds. In a separate bowl, whisk together the melted coconut oil, coconut cream, erythritol, vanilla extract, cinnamon, and a pinch of salt until well combined. Pour the wet ingredients over the dry ingredients and stir until everything is evenly coated.
Grease the inside of your slow cooker pot with a little coconut oil. Spread the granola mixture evenly in the pot. Cover and cook on low for 2 hours, stirring every 30 minutes to prevent burning and ensure even toasting. Once done, turn off the slow cooker and let the granola cool completely inside. It will crisp up as it cools.

NUTRITIONAL INFORMATION

Per serving: 450 calories, 10g protein, 15g carbohydrates, 40g fat, 10g fiber, 0mg cholesterol, 50mg sodium, 300mg potassium.

Slow Cooker Bacon and Egg Stuffed Peppers

INGREDIENTS

- 4 large bell peppers, tops cut off and seeds removed
- 8 large eggs
- 1/2 cup heavy cream
- 1 cup shredded cheddar cheese
- 8 slices of bacon, cooked and crumbled
- 1/4 cup finely chopped onion
- 1/4 teaspoon salt
- 1/4 teaspoon black pepper
- Chopped fresh chives or parsley for garnish (optional)

 Prep Time: 20 min

 Cook Time: 3 hours

 Serves: 4

DIRECTIONS

In a bowl, whisk together eggs, heavy cream, salt, and black pepper. Stir in the shredded cheddar cheese, crumbled bacon, and chopped onion. Carefully fill each bell pepper with the egg mixture, leaving a little space at the top for the mixture to expand. Place the stuffed peppers upright in the slow cooker. Cover and cook on low for 3 hours, or until the eggs are set. Once done, carefully remove the stuffed peppers from the slow cooker. Garnish with chopped fresh chives or parsley, if desired, and serve warm.

NUTRITIONAL INFORMATION

Per serving: 390 calories, 25g protein, 10g carbohydrates, 30g fat, 2g fiber, 410mg cholesterol, 720mg sodium, 340mg potassium.

Keto Crockpot French Toast Casserole

INGREDIENTS

- 1 loaf keto-friendly bread, cut into 1-inch cubes (about 6 cups)
- 6 large eggs
- 1 cup unsweetened almond milk
- 1/2 cup heavy cream
- 1/4 cup erythritol (or other keto-friendly sweetener)
- 1 teaspoon vanilla extract
- 1 teaspoon ground cinnamon
- 1/2 teaspoon nutmeg
- 1/4 teaspoon salt
- 1/2 cup chopped pecans (optional for topping)
- Butter for greasing

 Prep Time: 15 min

 Cook Time: 2.5 hours

 Serves: 4

DIRECTIONS

Grease the inside of your slow cooker pot with butter. Place the cubed keto-friendly bread in the slow cooker. In a large bowl, whisk together the eggs, almond milk, heavy cream, erythritol, vanilla extract, cinnamon, nutmeg, and salt until well combined. Pour the egg mixture over the bread cubes, pressing down lightly to ensure all the bread is soaked. Sprinkle the top with chopped pecans, if using. Cover and cook on low for 2.5 hours, or until the casserole is set and the top is slightly golden. Serve warm, optionally with a drizzle of keto-friendly syrup or a dusting of powdered erythritol.

NUTRITIONAL INFORMATION

Per serving: 350 calories, 18g protein, 10g carbohydrates, 26g fat, 5g fiber, 310mg cholesterol, 540mg sodium, 200mg potassium.

Slow Cooker Spinach and Mushroom Breakfast Quiche

INGREDIENTS

- 6 large eggs
- 1 cup heavy cream
- 1 cup fresh spinach, chopped
- 1 cup mushrooms, sliced
- 1/2 cup feta cheese, crumbled
- 1/4 cup parmesan cheese, grated
- 1/2 teaspoon salt
- 1/4 teaspoon black pepper
- 1/4 teaspoon garlic powder
- Non-stick cooking spray or butter for greasing

Prep Time: 15 min

Cook Time: 3 hours

Serves: 4

DIRECTIONS

Grease the inside of your slow cooker pot with non-stick cooking spray or butter. In a large bowl, whisk together eggs, heavy cream, salt, black pepper, and garlic powder until well combined. Stir in the chopped spinach, sliced mushrooms, crumbled feta cheese, and grated parmesan cheese. Mix until all ingredients are evenly distributed. Pour the mixture into the greased slow cooker pot. Cover and cook on low for 3 hours, or until the quiche is set and the edges are slightly golden. Once cooked, let the quiche stand for a few minutes before slicing. Serve warm.

NUTRITIONAL INFORMATION

Per serving: 390 calories, 20g protein, 5g carbohydrates, 33g fat, 1g fiber, 355mg cholesterol, 710mg sodium, 300mg potassium.

Lunch

Slow Cooker Buffalo Chicken Lettuce Wraps

INGREDIENTS

- 2 lbs chicken breast
- 1/2 cup buffalo sauce
- 1/4 cup chicken broth
- 1 tablespoon ranch seasoning mix
- 1 tablespoon olive oil
- 1 head of iceberg or butter lettuce, leaves separated for wraps
- 1/2 cup diced celery
- 1/2 cup shredded carrots
- 1/4 cup blue cheese crumbles

 Prep Time: 10 min

 Cook Time: 4 hours

 Serves: 4

DIRECTIONS

Place chicken breasts in the slow cooker. In a small bowl, mix together buffalo sauce, chicken broth, ranch seasoning, and olive oil. Pour the mixture over the chicken. Cover and cook on low for 4 hours, or until chicken is tender and can be easily shredded with a fork. Remove chicken from the slow cooker and shred using two forks. Return the shredded chicken to the slow cooker and stir well to coat with the sauce. To assemble the lettuce wraps, place a generous amount of buffalo chicken on a lettuce leaf, top with diced celery, shredded carrots, and blue cheese crumbles. Serve immediately, offering additional buffalo sauce on the side if desired.

NUTRITIONAL INFORMATION

Per serving: 350 calories, 38g protein, 5g carbohydrates, 18g fat, 2g fiber, 105mg cholesterol, 1200mg sodium, 400mg potassium.

Keto Beef Taco Soup

INGREDIENTS

- 2 pounds ground beef, browned and drained
- 1 (10-ounce) can diced tomatoes with green chilies, undrained
- 1 (4-ounce) can chopped green chilies
- 1 large onion, chopped
- 3 cloves garlic, minced
- 2 cups beef broth
- 1 tablespoon chili powder
- 1 teaspoon cumin
- 1 teaspoon salt
- 1/2 teaspoon black pepper

 Prep Time: 15 minutes

 Cook Time: 6 hours

 Serves: 6

DIRECTIONS

In the slow cooker, combine the browned ground beef, diced tomatoes with green chilies, chopped green chilies, onion, garlic, beef broth, chili powder, cumin, salt, and black pepper. Cover and cook on low for 6 hours to blend the flavors together. Serve hot, garnished with shredded cheddar cheese, a dollop of sour cream, and chopped fresh cilantro.

NUTRITIONAL INFORMATION

Per serving: 330 calories, 28g protein, 6g carbohydrates, 22g fat, 1g fiber, 85mg cholesterol, 790mg sodium, 300mg potassium.

Creamy Cauliflower Bacon Soup

INGREDIENTS

- 1 large head of cauliflower, cut into florets
- 6 slices of bacon, chopped
- 1 medium onion, diced
- 3 cloves garlic, minced
- 4 cups chicken broth
- 1 cup heavy cream
- 1 teaspoon salt
- 1/2 teaspoon black pepper
- 1/2 teaspoon paprika
- 1 cup shredded cheddar cheese
- Green onions for garnish

Prep Time: 15 min   Cook Time: 4 hours   Serves: 4

DIRECTIONS

In a skillet over medium heat, cook the chopped bacon until crisp. Remove bacon and set aside, reserving 2 tablespoons of bacon fat in the skillet. Add the diced onion and minced garlic to the skillet, sautéing until the onion is translucent. Place the cauliflower florets in the slow cooker. Add the sautéed onion and garlic, chicken broth, salt, pepper, and paprika. Stir to combine.

Cover and cook on low for 4 hours, or until the cauliflower is tender. Use an immersion blender to puree the soup until smooth (or carefully transfer to a blender in batches). Stir in the heavy cream and shredded cheddar cheese until the cheese is melted and the soup is well combined. Serve hot, garnished with crisp bacon pieces and chopped green onions.

NUTRITIONAL INFORMATION

Per serving: 420 calories, 15g protein, 12g carbohydrates, 36g fat, 3g fiber, 110mg cholesterol, 1300mg sodium, 500mg potassium.

Crockpot Jalapeño Popper Chicken Salad

INGREDIENTS

- 2 lbs boneless, skinless chicken breasts
- 1/2 cup chicken broth
- 1 teaspoon garlic powder
- 1 teaspoon onion powder
- 1/2 teaspoon black pepper
- 2 jalapeños, seeded and chopped
- 8 oz cream cheese, softened
- 1 cup shredded sharp cheddar cheese
- 1/2 cup mayonnaise
- 1/4 cup cooked and crumbled bacon

 Prep Time: 15 min

 Cook Time: 4 hours

 Serves: 4

DIRECTIONS

Place chicken breasts in slow cooker. Add chicken broth, garlic powder, onion powder, salt, and black pepper. Cook on low for 4 hours until chicken is tender. Remove, shred with forks. Drain excess liquid. Return shredded chicken to slow cooker. Add jalapeños, cream cheese, shredded cheddar, mayonnaise, and half of the bacon. Stir well. Cook on low for 30 minutes until cheese is melted. Serve warm, garnish with green onions and remaining bacon.

NUTRITIONAL INFORMATION

Per serving: 640 calories, 53g protein, 4g carbohydrates, 46g fat, 1g fiber, 190mg cholesterol, 950mg sodium, 400mg potassium.

Slow Cooked Zucchini Lasagna

INGREDIENTS

- 4 large zucchini, sliced lengthwise into thin strips
- 1 lb ground beef
- 1 cup ricotta cheese
- 1 cup shredded mozzarella cheese
- 1/2 cup grated Parmesan cheese
- 1 egg
- 24 oz marinara sauce (sugar-free for keto)
- 1 tablespoon olive oil
- 1 teaspoon garlic powder
- 1 teaspoon dried oregano
- 1/2 teaspoon salt
- 1/4 teaspoon black pepper

Prep Time: 25 min

Cook Time: 4 hours

Serves: 4

DIRECTIONS

Heat olive oil in a skillet over medium heat. Add ground beef, salt, and pepper, cooking until browned. Drain excess fat. In a bowl, mix ricotta cheese, Parmesan cheese, egg, garlic powder, and oregano. In the slow cooker, spread a thin layer of marinara sauce. Add a layer of zucchini slices, followed by a layer of the cooked ground beef, a layer of the cheese mixture, and a layer of mozzarella cheese. Repeat layers until all ingredients are used, finishing with a cheese layer. Cover and cook on low for 4 hours, or until the zucchini is tender and the lasagna is cooked through. Serve hot, garnished with fresh basil leaves.

NUTRITIONAL INFORMATION

Per serving: 540 calories, 38g protein, 12g carbohydrates, 38g fat, 3g fiber, 180mg cholesterol, 980mg sodium, 800mg potassium.

Crockpot Keto Chicken Caesar Salad

INGREDIENTS

- 2 lbs boneless, skinless chicken breasts
- 1/2 cup Caesar dressing, plus more for serving
- 1/4 cup water
- 1 teaspoon garlic powder
- 1 teaspoon onion powder
- Salt and pepper to taste
- 8 cups chopped romaine lettuce
- 1/2 cup grated Parmesan cheese
- 1/4 cup bacon bits
- 2 avocados, diced
- Lemon wedges for serving

 Prep Time: 10 min

 Cook Time: 4 hours

Serves: 4

DIRECTIONS

Place the chicken breasts in the slow cooker. In a small bowl, mix together the Caesar dressing, water, garlic powder, and onion powder. Pour over the chicken. Season with salt and pepper. Cover and cook on low for 4 hours, or until the chicken is fully cooked and tender. Once cooked, remove the chicken from the slow cooker and let it cool slightly before shredding with two forks.

In a large salad bowl, toss the chopped romaine lettuce with the shredded chicken, additional Caesar dressing to taste, grated Parmesan cheese, bacon bits, and diced avocados. Serve the salad with lemon wedges on the side.

NUTRITIONAL INFORMATION

Per serving: 550 calories, 45g protein, 8g carbohydrates, 38g fat, 7g fiber, 120mg cholesterol, 700mg sodium, 800mg potassium.

Slow Cooker Creamy Tomato Basil Soup

INGREDIENTS

- 2 cans (28 ounces each) whole peeled tomatoes
- 1 cup chicken or vegetable broth
- 1/2 cup chopped onion
- 3 cloves garlic, minced
- 1 teaspoon salt
- 1/2 teaspoon black pepper
- 1/2 teaspoon dried oregano
- 1/4 teaspoon crushed red pepper flakes (optional)
- 1 cup heavy cream
- 1/2 cup freshly grated Parmesan cheese
- 1/4 cup fresh basil leaves, chopped, plus more for garnish

Prep Time: 15 min

Cook Time: 6 hours

Serves: 4

DIRECTIONS

In the slow cooker, combine whole peeled tomatoes (with their juice), broth, onion, garlic, salt, black pepper, oregano, and red pepper flakes if using. Stir to mix well. Cover and cook on low for 6 hours, until the onions are soft and the flavors have melded together. Use an immersion blender to puree the soup until smooth (or carefully transfer to a blender in batches). Stir in the heavy cream, Parmesan cheese, and chopped basil. Cover and cook on low for an additional 30 minutes, or until the soup is heated through and the cheese has melted. Serve hot, garnished with additional basil leaves.

NUTRITIONAL INFORMATION

Per serving: 290 calories, 8g protein, 15g carbohydrates, 22g fat, 3g fiber, 80mg cholesterol, 900mg sodium, 700mg potassium.

Crockpot Lemon Thyme Chicken Soup

INGREDIENTS

- 2 lbs boneless, skinless chicken breasts
- 6 cups chicken broth
- 1 onion, diced
- 2 carrots, peeled and sliced
- 2 stalks of celery, sliced
- 3 cloves garlic, minced
- Juice of 2 lemons
- Zest of 1 lemon
- 1 teaspoon dried thyme
- Salt and pepper to taste
- 1/4 cup fresh parsley, chopped

Prep Time: 15 min

Cook Time: 6 hours

Serves: 4

DIRECTIONS

Place the chicken breasts in the slow cooker. Add the diced onion, sliced carrots, sliced celery, and minced garlic. Pour in the chicken broth. Add the lemon juice, lemon zest, dried thyme, salt, and pepper. Stir to combine all the ingredients. Cover and cook on low for 6 hours, or until the chicken is cooked through and the vegetables are tender. Remove the chicken from the slow cooker and shred it with two forks. Return the shredded chicken to the soup. Stir in the chopped fresh parsley. Serve hot, adjusting the seasoning with more salt, pepper, or lemon juice as needed.

NUTRITIONAL INFORMATION

Per serving: 260 calories, 35g protein, 8g carbohydrates, 8g fat, 2g fiber, 85mg cholesterol, 700mg sodium, 500mg potassium.

Keto Slow Cooker Pulled Pork Salad

INGREDIENTS

- 2 lbs pork shoulder
- 1 tablespoon smoked paprika
- 1 teaspoon garlic, onion powder
- 1/2 teaspoon cayenne pepper (adjust to taste)
- 1/4 cup apple cider vinegar
- 1/4 cup water
- 6 cups mixed salad greens
- 1 avocado, sliced
- 1/2 cup cherry tomatoes, halved
- 1/4 cup red onion, thinly sliced, 1/4 cup olive oil
- 2 tablespoons lemon juice
- 1 teaspoon Dijon mustard

 Prep Time: 20 min   Cook Time: 8 hours   Serves: 4

DIRECTIONS

Rub pork shoulder with smoked paprika, garlic powder, onion powder, cayenne pepper, salt, and black pepper. Place in slow cooker, add apple cider vinegar and water. Cook on low for 8 hours until tender. Shred pork, discard excess fat. In a salad bowl, combine greens, avocado, cherry tomatoes, and red onion. In a small bowl, whisk olive oil, lemon juice, Dijon mustard, salt, and pepper for dressing. Add shredded pork to salad, drizzle dressing, toss gently. Serve immediately for a well-mixed portion.

NUTRITIONAL INFORMATION

Per serving: 550 calories, 40g protein, 9g carbohydrates, 40g fat, 6g fiber, 115mg cholesterol, 320mg sodium, 800mg potassium.

Slow Cooker Beef and Broccoli

INGREDIENTS

- 1.5 lbs beef flank steak, thinly sliced against the grain
- 1 cup beef broth
- 1/2 cup soy sauce
- 3 tablespoons erythritol (or another keto-friendly sweetener)
- 2 tablespoons sesame oil
- 4 cloves garlic, minced
- 2 tablespoons ginger, grated
- 4 cups broccoli florets
- 2 teaspoons xanthan gum (optional)

 Prep Time: 15 min   Cook Time: 6 hours   Serves: 4

DIRECTIONS

In the slow cooker, whisk together beef broth, soy sauce (or coconut aminos), erythritol, sesame oil, garlic, and ginger. Add the thinly sliced beef and stir to coat. Cover and cook on low for 5 hours, or until the beef is tender. In the last hour of cooking, stir in the broccoli florets. If you're using xanthan gum to thicken the sauce, sprinkle it over the mixture and stir well to combine. Cover and cook for another hour, or until the broccoli is tender and the sauce has thickened to your liking. Serve the beef and broccoli garnished with sesame seeds and sliced green onions.

NUTRITIONAL INFORMATION

Per serving: 400 calories, 35g protein, 10g carbohydrates, 25g fat, 3g fiber, 90mg cholesterol, 1200mg sodium, 700mg potassium.

Crockpot Chicken Fajita Soup

INGREDIENTS

- 2 lbs boneless, skinless chicken breasts
- 3 cups chicken broth
- 1 medium onion, sliced
- 1 red bell pepper, sliced
- 1 green bell pepper, sliced
- 1 jalapeño, seeded and minced
- 2 cloves garlic, minced
- 1 tablespoon chili powder
- 1 teaspoon cumin
- 1 teaspoon paprika
- 1/2 teaspoon salt
- 1/2 teaspoon black pepper
- 1 cup diced tomatoes

 Prep Time: 15 min

 Cook Time: 4 hours

 Serves: 4

DIRECTIONS

Place the chicken breasts in the bottom of the slow cooker. Add the chicken broth, onion, bell peppers, jalapeño (if using), garlic, chili powder, cumin, paprika, salt, and black pepper. Cover and cook on low for 4 hours, or until the chicken is cooked through and tender. Remove the chicken from the slow cooker and shred with two forks. Return the shredded chicken to the slow cooker. Stir in the diced tomatoes and heavy cream. Cover and cook on low for an additional 30 minutes, or until the soup is heated through. Serve the soup garnished with fresh cilantro, avocado slices, and a dollop of sour cream if desired.

NUTRITIONAL INFORMATION

Per serving: 360 calories, 38g protein, 12g carbohydrates, 18g fat, 3g fiber, 105mg cholesterol, 800mg sodium, 700mg potassium.

Slow Cooker Spicy Shrimp Soup

INGREDIENTS

- 1 lb large shrimp, peeled and deveined
- 4 cups seafood or chicken broth
- 1 can (14.5 ounces) diced tomatoes, undrained
- 1 medium onion, chopped
- 2 celery stalks, chopped
- 1 bell pepper, chopped
- 2 garlic cloves, minced
- 1 jalapeño, seeded and minced
- 1 teaspoon chili powder, cumin
- 1/2 teaspoon smoked paprika

 Prep Time: 20 min

 Cook Time: 4 hours

 Serves: 4

DIRECTIONS

Add the broth, diced tomatoes, onion, celery, bell pepper, garlic, jalapeño, chili powder, cumin, and smoked paprika to the slow cooker. Stir to combine.
Cover and cook on low for 3.5 hours, allowing the flavors to meld. Add the shrimp to the slow cooker, season with salt and pepper, and stir. Cover and cook on low for an additional 30 minutes, or just until the shrimp are pink and cooked through. Stir in the fresh cilantro and lime juice just before serving. Serve the soup hot, with additional lime wedges on the side if desired.

NUTRITIONAL INFORMATION

Per serving: 180 calories, 24g protein, 8g carbohydrates, 4g fat, 2g fiber, 143mg cholesterol, 870mg sodium, 350mg potassium.

Crockpot Mediterranean Vegetable Stew

INGREDIENTS

- 1 large eggplant, cubed
- 2 zucchinis, cubed
- 2 bell pepper, chopped
- 1 large onion, chopped
- 3 cloves garlic, minced
- 1 can (28 ounces) diced tomatoes
- 1/4 cup olive oil
- 1 teaspoon dried oregano, dried basil
- 1/4 teaspoon black pepper
- 1/2 cup Kalamata olives, pitted and halved
- 1/4 cup capers, rinsed
- 1/4 cup fresh parsley, chopped

Prep Time: 20 minutes

Cook Time: 6 hours

Serves: 4

DIRECTIONS

In the slow cooker, combine the eggplant, zucchinis, bell peppers, onion, garlic, and diced tomatoes. Drizzle with olive oil and sprinkle with oregano, basil, salt, and black pepper. Stir to mix well. Cover and cook on low for 6 hours, or until vegetables are tender. Stir in Kalamata olives and capers in the last 30 minutes of cooking. Once cooked, adjust seasoning to taste, and stir in the fresh parsley just before serving. Serve warm as a hearty stew or over a bed of cauliflower rice for a complete meal.

NUTRITIONAL INFORMATION

Per serving: 220 calories, 4g protein, 18g carbohydrates, 15g fat, 8g fiber, 0mg cholesterol, 800mg sodium, 750mg potassium.

Slow Cooker Keto Clam Chowder

INGREDIENTS

- 2 cans (6.5 ounces each) chopped clams, juice reserved
- 1 cup cauliflower, chopped into small florets
- 1/2 cup celery, diced
- 1/2 cup onion, diced
- 2 cloves garlic, minced
- 2 cups chicken broth
- 1 cup heavy cream
- 1/2 teaspoon xanthan gum (for thickening)
- 1/2 teaspoon thyme
- 2 tablespoons butter

Prep Time: 15 min

Cook Time: 4 hours

Serves: 4

DIRECTIONS

In the slow cooker, combine the reserved clam juice, chopped cauliflower, diced celery, diced onion, minced garlic, and chicken broth. Stir to mix well. Cover and cook on low for 4 hours, or until the vegetables are tender. Stir in the chopped clams, heavy cream, and butter. Sprinkle the xanthan gum over the soup, stirring well to incorporate and thicken the soup. Season with thyme, salt, and pepper. Cover and cook on high for an additional 30 minutes, or until the soup is heated through and slightly thickened. Serve hot, garnished with chopped fresh parsley.

NUTRITIONAL INFORMATION

Per serving: 280 calories, 16g protein, 8g carbohydrates, 20g fat, 2g fiber, 95mg cholesterol, 600mg sodium, 400mg potassium.

Crockpot Sausage and Peppers

INGREDIENTS

- 1.5 lbs Italian sausage (choose keto-friendly, sugar-free sausages)
- 2 bell peppers, sliced (mix of colors)
- 1 large onion, sliced
- 2 cloves garlic, minced
- 1 can (14.5 ounces) diced tomatoes, drained
- 1 teaspoon dried oregano
- 1 teaspoon dried basil
- Salt and pepper to taste
- 1/4 cup chicken broth

Prep Time: 10 min

Cook Time: 6 hours

Serves: 4

DIRECTIONS

Place the Italian sausages in the bottom of the slow cooker. Top with sliced bell peppers, onion, and minced garlic. Add the drained diced tomatoes. Sprinkle with dried oregano, dried basil, salt, and pepper. Pour the chicken broth over the top. Cover and cook on low for 6 hours, until the sausages are cooked through and the vegetables are tender. Serve the sausage and peppers with a slotted spoon to avoid excess liquid, optionally inside low-carb buns or over cauliflower rice for a complete meal.

NUTRITIONAL INFORMATION

Per serving: 480 calories, 24g protein, 10g carbohydrates, 38g fat, 3g fiber, 85mg cholesterol, 1200mg sodium, 500mg potassium.

Dinner

Slow Cooker Garlic Butter Chicken Thighs

INGREDIENTS

- 8 bone-in, skin-on chicken thighs
- 1/2 cup unsalted butter, melted
- 4 cloves garlic, minced
- 1 teaspoon dried thyme
- 1 teaspoon dried rosemary
- Salt and pepper to taste
- Fresh parsley, chopped for garnish

 Prep Time: 10 min

 Cook Time: 6 hours

 Serves: 4

DIRECTIONS

Season the chicken thighs with salt and pepper. Place them in the slow cooker. In a small bowl, mix together the melted butter, minced garlic, dried thyme, and dried rosemary. Pour this mixture over the chicken thighs in the slow cooker, ensuring each thigh is well coated. Cover and cook on low for 6 hours, or until the chicken is cooked through and tender. If desired, to crisp the skin, place the cooked chicken thighs under a broiler for 2-3 minutes or until the skin is crispy and golden. Garnish with fresh parsley before serving.

NUTRITIONAL INFORMATION

Per serving: 470 calories, 35g protein, 1g carbohydrates, 36g fat, 0g fiber, 220mg cholesterol, 300mg sodium, 400mg potassium.

Keto Crockpot Spaghetti Squash and Meatballs

INGREDIENTS

- 1 large spaghetti squash, halved and seeds removed
- 1 lb ground beef (or turkey for a lighter option)
- 1/4 cup almond flour
- 1/4 cup grated Parmesan cheese
- 1 egg
- 2 cloves garlic, minced
- 1 teaspoon Italian seasoning
- Salt and pepper to taste
- 2 cups low-carb marinara sauce
- 1/2 cup water
- Fresh basil for garnish

Prep Time: 20 min

Cook Time: 6 hours

Serves: 4

DIRECTIONS

In a bowl, mix together ground beef, almond flour, grated Parmesan, egg, minced garlic, Italian seasoning, salt, and pepper. Form into meatballs. Place the halved spaghetti squash cut-side down in the slow cooker. Arrange the meatballs around the squash. Pour the marinara sauce and water over the meatballs. Cover and cook on low for 6 hours, or until the meatballs are cooked through and the spaghetti squash is tender. Carefully remove the spaghetti squash from the slow cooker. Use a fork to scrape the inside of the squash, creating spaghetti-like strands. Serve the spaghetti squash topped with meatballs and sauce. Garnish with fresh basil before serving.

NUTRITIONAL INFORMATION

Per serving: 450 calories, 28g protein, 18g carbohydrates, 32g fat, 6g fiber, 120mg cholesterol, 800mg sodium, 700mg potassium.

Slow Cooked Beef Short Ribs in Red Wine Sauce

INGREDIENTS

- 2 lbs beef short ribs
- Salt and pepper to taste
- 1 tablespoon olive oil
- 1 medium onion, chopped
- 2 cloves garlic, minced
- 1 cup dry red wine (choose a keto-friendly option, such as a dry Cabernet Sauvignon)
- 1 cup beef broth
- 2 tablespoons tomato paste
- 1 teaspoon dried thyme
- 1 bay leaf

Prep Time: 20 min

Cook Time: 8 hours

Serves: 4

DIRECTIONS

Season the beef short ribs with salt and pepper. In a skillet over medium-high heat, heat the olive oil and brown the ribs on all sides. Transfer the ribs to the slow cooker. In the same skillet, add the chopped onion and garlic. Sauté until softened, then add the red wine to deglaze the pan, scraping up any browned bits. Add the beef broth, tomato paste, thyme, and bay leaf. Bring to a simmer, then pour over the ribs in the slow cooker. Cover and cook on low for 8 hours, or until the ribs are tender and falling off the bone. Remove the ribs and bay leaf from the slow cooker. If desired, skim off any excess fat from the sauce and adjust seasoning to taste. Serve the ribs with the sauce spooned over the top.

NUTRITIONAL INFORMATION

Per serving: 600 calories, 22g protein, 5g carbohydrates, 48g fat, 1g fiber, 120mg cholesterol, 400mg sodium, 600mg potassium.

Crockpot Lemon Garlic Butter Salmon

INGREDIENTS

- 4 salmon fillets (about 6 ounces each)
- Salt and pepper to taste
- 4 tablespoons unsalted butter
- 2 lemons, 1 thinly sliced and 1 juiced
- 4 cloves garlic, minced
- 1 tablespoon fresh dill, chopped (plus extra for garnish)
- 1/4 cup chicken or vegetable broth

Prep Time: 10 min

Cook Time: 2 hours

Serves: 4

DIRECTIONS

Season the salmon fillets with salt and pepper. Place a few lemon slices at the bottom of the slow cooker. In a small saucepan, melt the butter over medium heat. Add the minced garlic and cook for 1-2 minutes until fragrant. Remove from heat and stir in the lemon juice. Place the salmon fillets on top of the lemon slices in the slow cooker. Pour the garlic butter mixture over the salmon. Add the chicken or vegetable broth around the salmon. Sprinkle the chopped dill over the top. Cover and cook on low for 2 hours, or until the salmon is cooked through and flakes easily with a fork. Serve the salmon with the cooked lemon slices and a sprinkle of fresh dill on top.

NUTRITIONAL INFORMATION

Per serving: 350 calories, 34g protein, 3g carbohydrates, 23g fat, 0g fiber, 105mg cholesterol, 200mg sodium, 800mg potassium.

Slow Cooker Creamy Tuscan Chicken

INGREDIENTS

- 4 boneless, skinless chicken breasts
- Salt and pepper to taste
- 1 tablespoon olive oil
- 3 cloves garlic, minced
- 1 cup heavy cream
- 1/2 cup chicken broth
- 1 teaspoon Italian seasoning
- 1/2 cup sun-dried tomatoes, chopped
- 1/4 cup grated Parmesan cheese
- 2 cups spinach, chopped

Prep Time: 15 min

Cook Time: 4 hours

Serves: 4

DIRECTIONS

Season chicken with salt and pepper. Brown in olive oil in a skillet over medium heat for 2-3 minutes on each side. Transfer to slow cooker. In the same skillet, sauté garlic for 1 minute. Add heavy cream, chicken broth, Italian seasoning, and sun-dried tomatoes. Simmer and pour over chicken. Cook on low for 4 hours. Stir in Parmesan and spinach, cook on high for 5 minutes until sauce thickens. Serve chicken with creamy Tuscan sauce, garnish with Parmesan and basil.

NUTRITIONAL INFORMATION

Per serving: 490 calories, 35g protein, 8g carbohydrates, 36g fat, 1g fiber, 180mg cholesterol, 620mg sodium, 500mg potassium.

Crockpot Keto Jambalaya

INGREDIENTS

- 1 lb chicken thighs, cut into bite-sized pieces
- 1 lb andouille sausage, sliced
- 1 large bell pepper, diced
- 1 medium onion, 2 stalks celery, diced
- 3 cloves garlic, minced
- 1 can (14.5 oz) diced tomatoes, drained
- 1 cup chicken broth
- 2 teaspoons Cajun seasoning
- 1 teaspoon smoked paprika
- 1/2 teaspoon dried thyme, oregano
- 1 lb shrimp, peeled and deveined
- 2 cups cauliflower rice

Prep Time: 20 min

Cook Time: 5 hours

Serves: 4

DIRECTIONS

In the slow cooker, combine chicken thighs, andouille sausage, bell pepper, onion, celery, garlic, diced tomatoes, chicken broth, Cajun seasoning, smoked paprika, thyme, oregano, salt, and pepper. Stir to mix well. Cover and cook on low for 4 hours. Add the shrimp and cauliflower rice to the slow cooker, stirring to combine. Cover and cook on high for 1 hour, or until the shrimp are pink and cooked through, and the cauliflower rice is tender. Adjust seasoning if necessary. Serve the jambalaya hot, garnished with chopped green onions and parsley.

NUTRITIONAL INFORMATION

Per serving: 550 calories, 48g protein, 12g carbohydrates, 32g fat, 3g fiber, 220mg cholesterol, 1400mg sodium, 800mg potassium.

Slow Cooker Balsamic Glazed Pork Tenderloin

INGREDIENTS

- 2 lbs pork tenderloin
- Salt and pepper to taste
- 1/2 cup balsamic vinegar
- 1/4 cup chicken broth
- 2 tablespoons olive oil
- 3 cloves garlic, minced
- 2 tablespoons erythritol (or another keto-friendly sweetener)
- 1 teaspoon dried rosemary
- 1 teaspoon dried thyme
- 1/2 teaspoon dried oregano

 Prep Time: 10 min

 Cook Time: 4 hours

 Serves: 4

DIRECTIONS

Season the pork tenderloin with salt and pepper. Place it in the slow cooker.

In a small bowl, whisk together balsamic vinegar, chicken broth, olive oil, minced garlic, erythritol, rosemary, thyme, and oregano. Pour the mixture over the pork tenderloin. Cover and cook on low for 4 hours, or until the pork is tender and cooked through. Remove the pork from the slow cooker and let it rest for a few minutes before slicing. Meanwhile, pour the liquid from the slow cooker into a small saucepan and simmer until it's reduced by half and thickened into a glaze. Slice the pork and drizzle the balsamic glaze over the top before serving.

NUTRITIONAL INFORMATION

Per serving: 320 calories, 35g protein, 5g carbohydrates, 16g fat, 0g fiber, 110mg cholesterol, 320mg sodium, 600mg potassium.

Keto Crockpot Chili

INGREDIENTS

- 2 lbs ground beef
- 1 large onion, diced
- 2 cloves garlic, minced
- 1 green bell pepper, diced
- 1 red bell pepper, diced
- 1 can (14.5 ounces) diced tomatoes, undrained
- 2 tablespoons tomato paste
- 2 cups beef broth
- 3 tablespoons chili powder
- 1 tablespoon cumin
- 1 teaspoon smoked paprika
- Salt and pepper to taste

Prep Time: 20 min   Cook Time: 8 hours   Serves: 6

DIRECTIONS

In a skillet over medium heat, brown the ground beef with the onion and garlic until the beef is no longer pink. Drain any excess fat. Transfer the beef mixture to the slow cooker. Add the green and red bell peppers, diced tomatoes with their juice, tomato paste, beef broth, chili powder, cumin, smoked paprika, salt, and pepper. Stir to combine. Cover and cook on low for 8 hours, allowing the flavors to meld together. Before serving, adjust the seasoning if necessary. Serve garnished with chopped fresh cilantro and shredded cheddar cheese if desired.

NUTRITIONAL INFORMATION

Per serving: 330 calories, 28g protein, 8g carbohydrates, 20g fat, 2g fiber, 85mg cholesterol, 700mg sodium, 750mg potassium.

Slow Cooker Moroccan Lamb Stew

INGREDIENTS

- 2 lbs lamb shoulder, cut into 1-inch pieces
- 2 tablespoons olive oil
- 1 large onion, chopped
- 3 cloves garlic, minced
- 1 teaspoon ground cumin
- 1 teaspoon ground cinnamon
- 1/2 teaspoon ground ginger
- 1/4 teaspoon cayenne pepper
- 1 can (14.5 ounces) diced tomatoes
- 1 cup beef broth
- 1 cup green olives, pitted
- 1/2 cup dried apricots, chopped

Prep Time: 20 min

Cook Time: 8 hours

Serves: 4

DIRECTIONS

Season the lamb pieces with salt and pepper. In a skillet over medium-high heat, heat the olive oil and brown the lamb on all sides. Transfer the lamb to the slow cooker. In the same skillet, add the onion and garlic, sautéing until softened. Add the cumin, cinnamon, ginger, and cayenne pepper, cooking for an additional minute until fragrant. Transfer this mixture to the slow cooker.

Add the diced tomatoes, beef broth, green olives, and dried apricots to the slow cooker, stirring to combine. Cover and cook on low for 8 hours, until the lamb is tender. Before serving, stir in the chopped cilantro and parsley. Adjust seasoning with salt and pepper if necessary.

NUTRITIONAL INFORMATION

Per serving: 520 calories, 38g protein, 22g carbohydrates, 34g fat, 4g fiber, 110mg cholesterol, 800mg sodium, 900mg potassium.

Crockpot Bacon-Wrapped Chicken Breast

INGREDIENTS

- 4 boneless, skinless chicken breasts
- 8 slices of bacon
- 1 teaspoon garlic powder
- 1 teaspoon smoked paprika
- Salt and pepper to taste
- 1/2 cup chicken broth
- 2 tablespoons olive oil
- 1 tablespoon fresh thyme, chopped

Prep Time: 15 min   Cook Time: 4 hours   Serves: 4

DIRECTIONS

Season the chicken breasts with garlic powder, smoked paprika, salt, and pepper. Wrap each chicken breast with 2 slices of bacon, securing with toothpicks if necessary. Heat olive oil in a skillet over medium-high heat. Sear each bacon-wrapped chicken breast on all sides until the bacon is crispy, about 2 minutes per side. Place the seared bacon-wrapped chicken breasts into the slow cooker. Pour chicken broth around the chicken. Sprinkle the fresh thyme over the top. Cover and cook on low for 4 hours, or until the chicken is cooked through and tender. Serve hot, removing toothpicks before serving.

NUTRITIONAL INFORMATION

Per serving: 410 calories, 55g protein, 1g carbohydrates, 20g fat, 0g fiber, 150mg cholesterol, 690mg sodium, 400mg potassium.

Slow Cooker Herbed Chicken and Vegetables

INGREDIENTS

- 4 boneless, skinless chicken breasts
- 1 tablespoon olive oil
- 1 teaspoon salt
- 1/2 teaspoon black pepper
- 1 teaspoon dried thyme
- 1 teaspoon dried rosemary
- 1 teaspoon garlic powder
- 2 cups cauliflower florets
- 1 cup broccoli florets
- 1 cup sliced zucchini
- 1/2 cup chicken broth

 Prep Time: 20 min Cook Time: 6 hours Serves: 4

DIRECTIONS

Rub the chicken breasts with olive oil and season with salt, pepper, thyme, rosemary, and garlic powder. Place the seasoned chicken breasts in the bottom of the slow cooker. Arrange the cauliflower, broccoli, and zucchini around and on top of the chicken. Pour the chicken broth over the vegetables and chicken. Cover and cook on low for 6 hours, or until the chicken is cooked through and the vegetables are tender. Serve hot, ensuring each plate has a generous portion of chicken and vegetables.

NUTRITIONAL INFORMATION

Per serving: 230 calories, 35g protein, 8g carbohydrates, 7g fat, 3g fiber, 85mg cholesterol, 650mg sodium, 500mg potassium.

Crockpot Coconut Lime Chicken

INGREDIENTS

- 4 boneless, skinless chicken breasts
- Salt and pepper to taste
- 1 can (14 ounces) coconut milk
- Juice and zest of 1 lime
- 2 cloves garlic, minced
- 1 tablespoon ginger, grated
- 1 teaspoon cumin
- 1/2 teaspoon chili flakes (adjust to taste)
- 1 tablespoon coconut oil
- Fresh cilantro for garnish

 Prep Time: 10 min Cook Time: 4 hours Serves: 4

DIRECTIONS

Season the chicken breasts with salt and pepper. In the slow cooker, whisk together the coconut milk, lime juice and zest, minced garlic, grated ginger, cumin, and chili flakes. Add the chicken breasts to the slow cooker, spooning the mixture over them to ensure they are well coated. Dot the top of the chicken with bits of coconut oil. Cover and cook on low for 4 hours, until the chicken is tender and cooked through. Serve the chicken garnished with fresh cilantro, with the sauce spooned over the top.

NUTRITIONAL INFORMATION

Per serving: 310 calories, 28g protein, 6g carbohydrates, 20g fat, 1g fiber, 75mg cholesterol, 200mg sodium, 400mg potassium.

Slow Cooker Spicy Beef Curry

INGREDIENTS

- 2 lbs beef chuck
- 2 tablespoons coconut oil
- 1 large onion, chopped
- 3 cloves garlic, minced
- 1 tablespoon ginger, grated
- 2 tablespoons curry powder
- 1 teaspoon turmeric
- 1/2 teaspoon cayenne pepper
- 14 ounces coconut milk
- 14 ounces diced tomatoes
- 1 tablespoon tomato paste
- 1 cinnamon stick
- 2 bay leaves

 Prep Time: 20 min

 Cook Time: 8 hours

 Serves: 4

DIRECTIONS

Season beef cubes with salt and pepper. Brown in coconut oil in a skillet over medium-high heat, then transfer to slow cooker. In the same skillet, cook onion, garlic, and ginger until onion is softened. Add curry powder, turmeric, and cayenne, cook for a minute. Stir in tomato paste, transfer to slow cooker. Add coconut milk, diced tomatoes, cinnamon stick, and bay leaves. Stir, cover, and cook on low for 8 hours until beef is tender and sauce thickens. Remove cinnamon stick and bay leaves. Serve curry garnished with fresh cilantro.

NUTRITIONAL INFORMATION

Per serving: 510 calories, 44g protein, 12g carbohydrates, 34g fat, 3g fiber, 135mg cholesterol, 200mg sodium, 900mg potassium.

Crockpot Italian Sausage and Peppers

INGREDIENTS

- 1.5 lbs Italian sausage (choose keto-friendly sausages)
- 2 bell peppers, sliced (any color)
- 1 large onion, sliced
- 3 cloves garlic, minced
- 1 can (14.5 ounces) diced tomatoes, drained
- 1 teaspoon dried oregano
- 1 teaspoon dried basil
- Salt and pepper to taste
- 1/4 cup olive oil

 Prep Time: 10 min

 Cook Time: 6 hours

 Serves: 4

DIRECTIONS

Place the Italian sausages in the slow cooker. Top with sliced bell peppers, onions, and minced garlic. Add the drained diced tomatoes. Sprinkle with oregano, basil, salt, and pepper. Drizzle olive oil over the top. Cover and cook on low for 6 hours, until the sausages are cooked through and the vegetables are tender. Serve hot, with the sausages and peppers drizzled with the cooking juices.

NUTRITIONAL INFORMATION

Per serving: 560 calories, 22g protein, 12g carbohydrates, 48g fat, 3g fiber, 95mg cholesterol, 1100mg sodium, 650mg potassium.

Slow Cooker Lemon Pepper Turkey Breast

INGREDIENTS

- 1 turkey breast (about 3 lbs), bone-in, skin-on
- 2 tablespoons olive oil
- 1 tablespoon lemon pepper seasoning
- 1 teaspoon garlic powder
- 1/2 teaspoon dried thyme
- Salt to taste
- 1 lemon, thinly sliced
- 1/2 cup chicken broth

Prep Time: 15 min

Cook Time: 7 hours

Serves: 4

DIRECTIONS

Rub the turkey breast with olive oil. In a small bowl, mix together the lemon pepper seasoning, garlic powder, dried thyme, and salt. Rub this seasoning mix all over the turkey breast. Place the lemon slices at the bottom of the slow cooker. Place the seasoned turkey breast on top of the lemon slices. Pour the chicken broth around the turkey in the slow cooker. Cover and cook on low for 7 hours, or until the turkey breast is cooked through and reaches an internal temperature of 165°F (74°C). Carefully remove the turkey breast from the slow cooker and let it rest for 10 minutes before slicing. Serve with the cooked lemon slices and a spoonful of the cooking juices drizzled over the top.

NUTRITIONAL INFORMATION

Per serving: 340 calories, 48g protein, 2g carbohydrates, 15g fat, 0g fiber, 125mg cholesterol, 320mg sodium, 500mg potassium.

Side Dishes

Cheesy Cauliflower Mash

INGREDIENTS

- 1 large head cauliflower, cut into florets
- 3 cloves garlic, peeled
- 1/2 cup chicken or vegetable broth
- 1/2 cup heavy cream
- 1 cup shredded cheddar cheese
- 2 tablespoons unsalted butter
- Salt and pepper to taste
- Fresh chives, chopped for garnish

 Prep Time: 10 min

 Cook Time: 3 hours

 Serves: 4

DIRECTIONS

Place cauliflower florets and garlic cloves in the slow cooker. Pour broth over the top. Cover and cook on high for 3 hours, or until the cauliflower is very tender. Drain any excess liquid from the slow cooker. Add heavy cream, cheddar cheese, and butter to the cauliflower. Use an immersion blender to blend the cauliflower mixture until smooth and creamy. Alternatively, you can transfer the mixture to a food processor or blender. Season with salt and pepper to taste. Serve the cauliflower mash hot, garnished with chopped chives.

NUTRITIONAL INFORMATION

Per serving: 250 calories, 9g protein, 8g carbohydrates, 20g fat, 3g fiber, 60mg cholesterol, 320mg sodium, 430mg potassium.

Crockpot Garlic Parmesan Green Beans

INGREDIENTS

- 1.5 lbs fresh green beans, trimmed
- 3 tablespoons olive oil
- 4 cloves garlic, minced
- 1/2 cup chicken broth
- 1/2 cup grated Parmesan cheese
- Salt and pepper to taste
- Additional grated Parmesan cheese for serving

 Prep Time: 10 min

 Cook Time: 2.5 hours

 Serves: 4

DIRECTIONS

Place the green beans in the slow cooker. In a small bowl, mix together the olive oil and minced garlic. Pour this mixture over the green beans, tossing to coat evenly. Pour chicken broth over the green beans. Season with salt and pepper. Cover and cook on high for 2.5 hours, or until the green beans are tender but still crisp. Just before serving, sprinkle with grated Parmesan cheese and toss to combine. Serve hot, topped with additional Parmesan cheese if desired.

NUTRITIONAL INFORMATION

Per serving: 180 calories, 7g protein, 10g carbohydrates, 12g fat, 4g fiber, 15mg cholesterol, 320mg sodium, 350mg potassium.

Slow Cooker Spiced Brussels Sprouts

INGREDIENTS

- 1.5 lbs Brussels sprouts, trimmed and halved
- 3 tablespoons olive oil
- 1 teaspoon garlic powder
- 1 teaspoon smoked paprika
- 1/2 teaspoon salt
- 1/4 teaspoon black pepper
- 1/4 teaspoon cayenne pepper (adjust to taste)
- 1/2 cup water

 Prep Time: 10 minutes

 Cook Time: 3 hours

 Serves: 4

DIRECTIONS

In a large bowl, toss the Brussels sprouts with olive oil, garlic powder, smoked paprika, salt, black pepper, and cayenne pepper until evenly coated. Transfer the seasoned Brussels sprouts to the slow cooker. Pour water into the bottom of the slow cooker. Cover and cook on high for 3 hours, or until the Brussels sprouts are tender but still slightly crisp. Stir the Brussels sprouts once or twice during cooking to ensure even seasoning and cooking. Serve hot, adjusting seasoning with additional salt and pepper if desired.

NUTRITIONAL INFORMATION

Per serving: 140 calories, 5g protein, 10g carbohydrates, 10g fat, 4g fiber, 0mg cholesterol, 300mg sodium, 450mg potassium.

Keto Creamed Spinach

INGREDIENTS

- 2 lbs fresh spinach, washed and trimmed
- 1 cup heavy cream
- 4 ounces cream cheese
- 2 cloves garlic, minced
- 1/2 teaspoon nutmeg
- Salt and pepper to taste
- 1/2 cup grated Parmesan cheese

 Prep Time: 10 min

 Cook Time: 2 hours

 Serves: 4

DIRECTIONS

Place the spinach in the slow cooker. Add the heavy cream, cream cheese, minced garlic, nutmeg, salt, and pepper. Cover and cook on low for 2 hours, stirring occasionally until the spinach is wilted and the cream cheese is fully melted into the cream, creating a smooth sauce. Before serving, stir in the grated Parmesan cheese until it's completely melted and mixed into the spinach. Adjust the seasoning with additional salt and pepper if needed. Serve hot as a side dish.

NUTRITIONAL INFORMATION

Per serving: 290 calories, 9g protein, 8g carbohydrates, 25g fat, 3g fiber, 90mg cholesterol, 430mg sodium, 580mg potassium.

Slow Cooked Bacon and Collard Greens

INGREDIENTS

- 1 lb bacon, chopped
- 2 lbs collard greens, stems removed and leaves chopped
- 1 onion, chopped
- 3 cloves garlic, minced
- 1 cup chicken broth
- 2 tablespoons apple cider vinegar
- 1 teaspoon red pepper flakes (adjust to taste)
- Salt and pepper to taste

Prep Time: 15 min   Cook Time: 6 hours   Serves: 4

DIRECTIONS

In a skillet over medium heat, cook chopped bacon until starting to crisp. Remove bacon, set aside, and reserve 2 tablespoons of bacon fat in the skillet. Add chopped onion and minced garlic to the skillet with reserved bacon fat. Sauté until onion is translucent. Transfer bacon, sautéed onion, and garlic to the slow cooker. Add chopped collard greens, chicken broth, apple cider vinegar, and red pepper flakes. Season with salt and pepper. Cover and cook on low for 6 hours until collard greens are tender. Stir well before serving to distribute bacon and seasonings.

NUTRITIONAL INFORMATION

Per serving: 400 calories, 15g protein, 10g carbohydrates, 34g fat, 6g fiber, 75mg cholesterol, 900mg sodium, 500mg potassium.

Crockpot Herbed Almond Bread

INGREDIENTS

- 2 cups almond flour
- 1 tablespoon coconut flour
- 1/4 cup ground flaxseed
- 1 teaspoon baking powder
- 1/2 teaspoon salt
- 4 large eggs
- 1/4 cup unsalted butter, melted
- 2 tablespoons olive oil
- 1 teaspoon apple cider vinegar
- 1 tablespoon fresh rosemary, finely chopped
- 1 tablespoon fresh thyme, finely chopped

Prep Time: 15 min   Cook Time: 2 hours   Serves: 4

DIRECTIONS:

In a large bowl, combine almond flour, coconut flour, ground flaxseed, baking powder, and salt. In another bowl, whisk together the eggs, melted butter, olive oil, and apple cider vinegar. Stir the wet ingredients into the dry ingredients until well combined. Fold in the chopped rosemary and thyme.
Line the slow cooker with parchment paper and pour the batter into the center. Spread evenly with a spatula. Cover and cook on high for 2 hours, or until a toothpick inserted into the center comes out clean. Lift the bread out of the slow cooker using the edges of the parchment paper. Let it cool before slicing.

NUTRITIONAL INFORMATION

Per serving: 480 calories, 18g protein, 12g carbohydrates, 42g fat, 6g fiber, 220mg cholesterol, 350mg sodium, 300mg potassium.

Slow Cooker Garlic Herb Mushrooms

INGREDIENTS

- 1.5 lbs fresh mushrooms, cleaned and stems trimmed
- 1/4 cup unsalted butter, melted
- 4 cloves garlic, minced
- 2 tablespoons olive oil
- 1 tablespoon fresh thyme, chopped
- 1 tablespoon fresh rosemary, chopped
- Salt and pepper to taste
- 1/4 cup chicken broth

 Prep Time: 10 min

 Cook Time: 3 hours

 Serves: 4

DIRECTIONS

In a large bowl, toss the mushrooms with the melted butter, minced garlic, olive oil, thyme, rosemary, salt, and pepper until the mushrooms are well coated. Transfer the mushroom mixture to the slow cooker. Pour the chicken broth over the mushrooms. Cover and cook on low for 3 hours, or until the mushrooms are tender and flavorful. Before serving, adjust seasoning if necessary and garnish with fresh parsley.

NUTRITIONAL INFORMATION

Per serving: 220 calories, 6g protein, 8g carbohydrates, 20g fat, 2g fiber, 30mg cholesterol, 200mg sodium, 500mg potassium.

Crockpot Keto Cauliflower "Potato" Salad

INGREDIENTS

- 1 large head cauliflower, cut into small florets
- 1/2 cup mayonnaise
- 2 tablespoons mustard
- 1/4 cup dill pickles, chopped
- 2 hard-boiled eggs, chopped
- 1/4 cup red onion, finely chopped
- 2 tablespoons fresh dill, chopped
- Salt and pepper to taste
- Paprika for garnish

 Prep Time: 15 min

 Cook Time: 3 hours

 Serves: 4

DIRECTIONS

Place cauliflower florets in the slow cooker. Add 1/4 cup water. Cover and cook on high for 2-3 hours, or until the cauliflower is tender but not mushy. Drain any excess liquid and let cool. In a large bowl, mix mayonnaise, mustard, dill pickles, chopped eggs, red onion, and fresh dill. Season with salt and pepper to taste. Once the cauliflower is cool, add it to the mayonnaise mixture. Gently fold everything together until the cauliflower is well coated.

Refrigerate for at least 1 hour before serving, allowing the flavors to meld. Serve chilled, garnished with a sprinkle of paprika.

NUTRITIONAL INFORMATION

Per serving: 240 calories, 7g protein, 8g carbohydrates, 20g fat, 3g fiber, 95mg cholesterol, 320mg sodium, 450mg potassium.

Slow Cooker Cheesy Jalapeño Cornbread

INGREDIENTS

- 1 1/2 cups almond flour
- 1/2 cup coconut flour
- 1 tablespoon baking powder
- 1/2 teaspoon salt
- 1/4 cup unsalted butter, melted
- 4 large eggs, beaten
- 1/2 cup almond milk
- 1 cup shredded cheddar cheese
- 2 jalapeños, seeded and finely chopped
- 1/4 cup sour cream (for serving, optional)

 Prep Time: 15 minutes

 Cook Time: 2 hours

 Serves: 6

DIRECTIONS

In a large bowl, whisk together almond flour, coconut flour, baking powder, and salt. Stir in melted butter, beaten eggs, and almond milk until well combined. Fold in shredded cheddar cheese and chopped jalapeños. Line the slow cooker with parchment paper or lightly grease it with butter. Pour the batter into the slow cooker and spread evenly. Cover and cook on high for 2 hours or until a toothpick inserted into the center comes out clean. Let the cornbread cool for a few minutes before slicing. Serve warm with a dollop of sour cream on top if desired.

NUTRITIONAL INFORMATION

Per serving: 320 calories, 14g protein, 12g carbohydrates, 26g fat, 6g fiber, 185mg cholesterol, 430mg sodium, 200mg potassium.

Crockpot Creamy Ranch Cauliflower

INGREDIENTS

- 1 large head cauliflower, cut into florets
- 1 cup chicken broth
- 1/2 cup heavy cream
- 1 packet ranch dressing mix (or 2 tablespoons homemade keto-friendly ranch seasoning)
- 1/2 cup shredded cheddar cheese
- 2 tablespoons unsalted butter
- Salt and pepper to taste
- Fresh chives, chopped for garnish

 Prep Time: 10 min

 Cook Time: 3 hours

 Serves: 4

DIRECTIONS

Place the cauliflower florets in the slow cooker. Pour the chicken broth over the cauliflower. Cover and cook on high for 2 hours, or until the cauliflower is tender. Drain any excess liquid from the slow cooker. Add the heavy cream, ranch dressing mix, shredded cheddar cheese, and butter to the cauliflower. Season with salt and pepper to taste. Cover and cook on high for an additional hour, stirring occasionally, until the cheese is melted and the mixture is creamy. Serve hot, garnished with chopped chives.

NUTRITIONAL INFORMATION

Per serving: 220 calories, 7g protein, 8g carbohydrates, 18g fat, 3g fiber, 60mg cholesterol, 750mg sodium, 450mg potassium.

Slow Cooker Cinnamon Roasted Nuts

INGREDIENTS

- 2 cups almonds
- 2 cups pecans
- 1/4 cup unsalted butter, melted
- 1/3 cup erythritol (or another keto-friendly sweetener)
- 2 teaspoons ground cinnamon
- 1/2 teaspoon salt
- 1 teaspoon vanilla extract

Prep Time: 10 min

Cook Time: 3 hours

Serves: 6

DIRECTIONS

In a large bowl, combine the almonds and pecans. Pour the melted butter over the nuts and stir to coat evenly. In a small bowl, mix together the erythritol, ground cinnamon, and salt. Sprinkle this mixture over the buttered nuts, add vanilla extract, and toss until the nuts are evenly coated. Line the slow cooker with parchment paper (for easy cleanup) and pour the nut mixture into the slow cooker. Cover and cook on low for 3 hours, stirring every hour to ensure even roasting. Spread the nuts out on a baking sheet to cool completely. They will become crunchier as they cool.

NUTRITIONAL INFORMATION

Per serving: 420 calories, 12g protein, 10g carbohydrates, 38g fat, 6g fiber, 0mg cholesterol, 200mg sodium, 400mg potassium.

Crockpot Spicy Cauliflower Rice

INGREDIENTS

- 1 large head cauliflower, riced (about 4 cups)
- 1 tablespoon olive oil
- 1 medium onion, diced
- 2 cloves garlic, minced
- 1 jalapeño, seeded and finely chopped
- 1 teaspoon cumin
- 1/2 teaspoon chili powder
- 1/2 teaspoon smoked paprika
- Salt and pepper to taste
- 1/2 cup vegetable broth
- 1/4 cup fresh cilantro, chopped
- Lime wedges for serving

Prep Time: 15 minutes

Cook Time: 2.5 hours

Serves: 4

DIRECTIONS

Pulse the cauliflower in a food processor until it resembles rice grains. In a skillet over medium heat, sauté onion, garlic, and jalapeño in olive oil until softened. Add cumin, chili powder, smoked paprika, salt, and pepper, cooking for another minute until fragrant. Transfer the sautéed vegetables to the slow cooker. Add the riced cauliflower and vegetable broth, stirring to combine. Cover and cook on high for 2.5 hours, or until the cauliflower is tender and the flavors have melded. Stir in fresh cilantro just before serving. Serve with lime wedges on the side.

NUTRITIONAL INFORMATION

Per serving: 90 calories, 3g protein, 12g carbohydrates, 4g fat, 4g fiber, 0mg cholesterol, 200mg sodium, 450mg potassium.

Slow Cooker Balsamic Roasted Vegetables

INGREDIENTS

- 2 zucchinis, cut into bite-sized pieces
- 2 bell peppers (any color), cut into bite-sized pieces
- 1 red onion, cut into wedges
- 1 cup cherry tomatoes
- 1/4 cup balsamic vinegar
- 2 tablespoons olive oil
- 2 cloves garlic, minced
- 1 teaspoon dried basil
- 1 teaspoon dried oregano
- Salt and pepper to taste
- Fresh parsley, chopped for garnish

Prep Time: 15 min   Cook Time: 4 hours   Serves: 4

DIRECTIONS

In a large bowl, combine zucchinis, bell peppers, red onion, and cherry tomatoes. In a small bowl, whisk together balsamic vinegar, olive oil, minced garlic, dried basil, dried oregano, salt, and pepper. Pour this mixture over the vegetables, tossing until they are well coated. Transfer the coated vegetables to the slow cooker. Cover and cook on low for 4 hours, or until the vegetables are tender but still hold their shape. Adjust the seasoning with additional salt and pepper if necessary. Serve hot, garnished with fresh parsley.

NUTRITIONAL INFORMATION

Per serving: 150 calories, 3g protein, 18g carbohydrates, 8g fat, 5g fiber, 0mg cholesterol, 150mg sodium, 600mg potassium.

Crockpot Smoky Bacon Greens

INGREDIENTS

- 1 lb smoked bacon, chopped
- 1 large onion, diced
- 3 cloves garlic, minced
- 2 lbs mixed greens (collard greens, mustard greens, kale), stems removed and leaves chopped
- 3 cups chicken broth
- 1 tablespoon apple cider vinegar
- 1 teaspoon red pepper flakes (adjust to taste)
- Salt and pepper to taste

Prep Time: 15 min

Cook Time: 4 hours

Serves: 4

DIRECTIONS

In a large skillet over medium heat, cook the chopped bacon until crisp. Remove bacon with a slotted spoon and set aside, leaving the bacon grease in the skillet. Add the diced onion and minced garlic to the skillet, and sauté until the onion is translucent and garlic is fragrant. Transfer the bacon, onion, and garlic to the slow cooker. Add the chopped greens, chicken broth, apple cider vinegar, and red pepper flakes. Season with salt and pepper. Cover and cook on low for 4 hours, until the greens are tender and flavorful. Stir well before serving, ensuring the bacon and all flavors are evenly distributed through the greens.

NUTRITIONAL INFORMATION

Per serving: 300 calories, 15g protein, 10g carbohydrates, 22g fat, 5g fiber, 50mg cholesterol, 900mg sodium, 600mg potassium.

Slow Cooker Lemon Asparagus

INGREDIENTS

- 2 lbs fresh asparagus, ends trimmed
- 2 tablespoons olive oil
- Juice and zest of 1 lemon
- 2 cloves garlic, minced
- Salt and pepper to taste
- Additional lemon slices for garnish

Prep Time: 5 min

Cook Time: 1.5 hours

Serves: 4

DIRECTIONS

Place the trimmed asparagus in the slow cooker. Drizzle with olive oil and sprinkle with the lemon juice, lemon zest, minced garlic, salt, and pepper. Toss gently to coat the asparagus evenly. Arrange the asparagus in a single layer as much as possible. Cover and cook on high for 1.5 hours, or until the asparagus is tender but still crisp. Once cooked, carefully remove the asparagus from the slow cooker to avoid overcooking. Serve immediately, garnished with additional lemon slices.

NUTRITIONAL INFORMATION

Per serving: 110 calories, 6g protein, 10g carbohydrates, 7g fat, 5g fiber, 0mg cholesterol, 200mg sodium, 400mg potassium.

Snacks and Small Bites

Crockpot Buffalo Chicken Dip

INGREDIENTS

- 2 cups cooked and shredded chicken
- 1 package (8 ounces) cream cheese, softened
- 1/2 cup ranch dressing
- 1/2 cup buffalo wing sauce
- 1 cup shredded cheddar cheese
- 1/2 cup crumbled blue cheese (optional)

Prep Time: 10 minutes

Cook Time: 2 hours

Serves: 6

DIRECTIONS

In the slow cooker, combine the shredded chicken, cream cheese, ranch dressing, and buffalo wing sauce. Stir until the mixture is well combined. Cover and cook on low for 2 hours, stirring occasionally, until the mixture is hot and the cheeses have melted. Stir in the shredded cheddar cheese (and blue cheese if using) until melted and smooth. Keep the dip on the "warm" setting (if available) to serve during gatherings. Serve with celery sticks, cucumber slices, or low-carb crackers for dipping.

NUTRITIONAL INFORMATION

Per serving: 350 calories, 22g protein, 3g carbohydrates, 28g fat, 0g fiber, 105mg cholesterol, 800mg sodium, 200mg potassium.

Slow Cooker Salted Caramel Pecan Pie

INGREDIENTS

- 2 cups pecans, chopped
- 1/4 cup unsalted butter, melted
- 1/3 cup erythritol (or another keto-friendly sweetener)
- 1/2 cup heavy cream
- 1 teaspoon vanilla extract
- 1/2 teaspoon sea salt, plus extra for sprinkling
- 2 eggs, beaten

Prep Time: 20 min

Cook Time: 3 hours

Serves: 4

DIRECTIONS

In a bowl, mix the pecans with the melted butter, erythritol, heavy cream, vanilla extract, sea salt, and beaten eggs until well combined. Line the slow cooker with parchment paper, leaving enough overhang to lift the pie out easily. Pour the pecan mixture into the lined slow cooker. Cover and cook on low for 3 hours, or until the mixture is set and the edges are slightly golden. The center should be just a bit jiggly as it will set further upon cooling. Turn off the slow cooker and let the pie cool completely before lifting it out using the parchment paper overhang. Sprinkle with a little more sea salt before serving.

NUTRITIONAL INFORMATION

Per serving: 470 calories, 8g protein, 10g carbohydrates, 45g fat, 5g fiber, 120mg cholesterol, 300mg sodium, 400mg potassium.

Keto Slow Cooker Cheddar Cheese Chips

INGREDIENTS

- 2 cups shredded cheddar cheese
- 1/2 teaspoon paprika (optional for flavor)
- 1/4 teaspoon garlic powder (optional for flavor)

 Prep Time: 5 minutes

 Cook Time: 1 hour

 Serves: 4

DIRECTIONS

Line the bottom of the slow cooker with parchment paper to prevent sticking.

Mix the shredded cheddar cheese with paprika and garlic powder if using, then spread the cheese in an even layer on the parchment paper. Cover and cook on high for about 1 hour, or until the cheese is fully melted and slightly golden around the edges. Carefully remove the parchment paper with the melted cheese from the slow cooker and place it on a baking sheet. Optional: For additional crispiness, place the baking sheet under the broiler in an oven for 2-3 minutes or until the cheese reaches desired crispiness. Watch closely to avoid burning. Let cool completely, then break into chip-sized pieces.

NUTRITIONAL INFORMATION

Per serving: 230 calories, 14g protein, 1g carbohydrates, 19g fat, 0g fiber, 60mg cholesterol, 350mg sodium, 0mg potassium.

Crockpot Spinach and Artichoke Dip

INGREDIENTS

- 1 package (10 ounces) frozen spinach, thawed and squeezed dry
- 1 can (14 ounces) artichoke hearts, drained and chopped
- 8 ounces cream cheese, cut into cubes
- 1 cup sour cream
- 1 cup shredded mozzarella cheese
- 1/2 cup grated Parmesan cheese
- 2 cloves garlic, minced
- 1/2 teaspoon salt
- 1/4 teaspoon black pepper

 Prep Time: 10 min

 Cook Time: 2 hours

 Serves: 6

DIRECTIONS

In the slow cooker, combine the spinach, chopped artichoke hearts, cubed cream cheese, sour cream, mozzarella cheese, Parmesan cheese, minced garlic, salt, and pepper. Stir to mix well. Cover and cook on low for 2 hours, stirring halfway through the cook time, until the cheeses are melted and the dip is hot and creamy. Stir the dip well before serving to ensure all ingredients are evenly distributed. Adjust seasoning with additional salt and pepper if desired. Serve the dip warm with low-carb vegetables, pork rinds, or keto-friendly crackers for dipping.

NUTRITIONAL INFORMATION

Per serving: 300 calories, 14g protein, 8g carbohydrates, 24g fat, 2g fiber, 70mg cholesterol, 580mg sodium, 300mg potassium.

Slow Cooker Jalapeño Cheddar Egg Bites

INGREDIENTS

- 8 large eggs
- 1/2 cup heavy cream
- 1 cup shredded cheddar cheese
- 1 jalapeño, finely diced (remove seeds for less heat)
- Salt and pepper to taste
- Cooking spray or oil for greasing

Prep Time: 15 min   Cook Time: 2 hours   Serves: 6

DIRECTIONS

In a large bowl, whisk together the eggs and heavy cream until well combined. Stir in the shredded cheddar cheese and diced jalapeño. Season with salt and pepper to taste. Grease silicone egg bite molds or small ramekins that will fit in your slow cooker. Pour the egg mixture into the molds, filling each about three-quarters full. Pour 1 cup of water into the bottom of the slow cooker and place a trivet or steamer rack inside. Carefully set the filled molds on the trivet.

Cover and cook on high for 2 hours, or until the egg bites are set and firm to the touch. Once done, remove the molds from the slow cooker and let them cool for a few minutes. Then, gently pop the egg bites out of the molds.

NUTRITIONAL INFORMATION

Per serving: 210 calories, 14g protein, 2g carbohydrates, 16g fat, 0g fiber, 285mg cholesterol, 320mg sodium, 150mg potassium.

Crockpot Keto Nachos

INGREDIENTS

- 1 lb ground beef
- 1 tablespoon taco seasoning (make sure it's sugar-free for keto)
- 1/2 cup water
- 1 cup cheddar cheese, shredded
- 1/2 cup pepper jack cheese, shredded
- 1/4 cup black olives, sliced
- 1/4 cup jalapeños, sliced
- 1/2 cup cherry tomatoes, quartered
- 1 avocado, diced
- 1/4 cup sour cream

Prep Time: 15 min

Cook Time: 4 hours

Serves: 4

DIRECTIONS

In the slow cooker, combine the ground beef, taco seasoning, and water. Break the meat apart with a spoon to mix well with the seasoning. Cover and cook on low for 4 hours, or until the beef is fully cooked. Drain any excess fat.

Sprinkle the cooked beef with cheddar and pepper jack cheese. Cover for an additional 10 minutes, or until the cheese is melted. Once the cheese is melted, top the meat and cheese mixture with black olives, jalapeños, and cherry tomatoes. Serve the keto nacho mixture with diced avocado and a dollop of sour cream on the side. Use keto-friendly chips or sliced bell peppers for dipping.

NUTRITIONAL INFORMATION

Per serving: 450 calories, 30g protein, 8g carbohydrates, 35g fat, 4g fiber, 120mg cholesterol, 600mg sodium, 400mg potassium.

Slow Cooker Bacon-Wrapped Little Smokies

INGREDIENTS

- 1 package (14 ounces) little smokies (ensure they're sugar-free for keto)
- 1 pound bacon, cut into thirds
- 1/2 cup keto-friendly brown sugar substitute (like erythritol or monk fruit sweetener)
- 1 tablespoon Dijon mustard (optional for glaze)
- 2 tablespoons apple cider vinegar (optional for glaze)
- Toothpicks

 Prep Time: 20 min

 Cook Time: 3 hours

 Serves: 6

DIRECTIONS

Wrap each little smokie with a piece of bacon and secure with a toothpick. Place in the slow cooker. In a small bowl, mix the keto-friendly brown sugar substitute with Dijon mustard and apple cider vinegar if using, to create a glaze. Pour this mixture over the bacon-wrapped smokies in the slow cooker.

Cover and cook on low for 3 hours, or until the bacon is cooked to your liking.

Once done, switch the slow cooker to the warm setting and serve directly from the pot for guests to enjoy. If you prefer a crispier bacon finish, transfer the cooked bacon-wrapped smokies to a baking sheet and broil in the oven for 2-3 minutes before serving.

NUTRITIONAL INFORMATION

Per serving: 350 calories, 20g protein, 2g carbohydrates, 30g fat, 0g fiber, 75mg cholesterol, 950mg sodium, 300mg potassium.

Crockpot Spicy Roasted Almonds

INGREDIENTS

- 3 cups raw almonds
- 1 tablespoon olive oil
- 1 teaspoon chili powder
- 1 teaspoon smoked paprika
- 1/2 teaspoon garlic powder
- 1/2 teaspoon onion powder
- 1/4 teaspoon cayenne pepper (adjust according to spice preference)
- Salt to taste

Prep Time: 5 min

Cook Time: 2 hours

Serves: 6

DIRECTIONS

In a large bowl, mix the almonds with olive oil until they are well coated. In a small bowl, combine the chili powder, smoked paprika, garlic powder, onion powder, cayenne pepper, and salt. Sprinkle this spice mixture over the almonds, tossing to ensure they are evenly coated. Line the slow cooker with parchment paper (for easy cleanup) and spread the seasoned almonds in an even layer. Cover and cook on low for 2 hours, stirring every 30 minutes to ensure even roasting. Once done, spread the almonds on a baking sheet to cool. They will become crunchier as they cool.

NUTRITIONAL INFORMATION

Per serving: 320 calories, 12g protein, 10g carbohydrates, 28g fat, 6g fiber, 0mg cholesterol, 200mg sodium, 400mg potassium.

Slow Cooker Cheesy Garlic Breadsticks

INGREDIENTS

- 2 cups shredded mozzarella cheese (divided)
- 1 cup almond flour
- 2 tablespoons cream cheese
- 1 egg
- 1 teaspoon garlic powder
- 1/2 teaspoon onion powder
- 1/2 teaspoon dried oregano
- 1/4 teaspoon salt
- 2 tablespoons unsalted butter, melted
- 1 clove garlic, minced
- Fresh parsley, chopped for garnish

Prep Time: 15 min

Cook Time: 1.5 hours

Serves: 4

DIRECTIONS

Combine 1 1/2 cups mozzarella, almond flour, and cream cheese in a microwave-safe bowl. Microwave for 60 seconds, stir, and microwave for 30 more seconds until melted. Add egg, garlic powder, onion powder, dried oregano, and salt. Mix to form a dough. Line slow cooker with parchment paper, press dough into the bottom. Brush with melted butter, sprinkle minced garlic on top. Cover and cook on high for 1-1.5 hours until edges are golden and center is set. Sprinkle remaining 1/2 cup mozzarella on top, cover for 10 more minutes until melted and bubbly. Garnish with fresh parsley, cut into sticks, and serve warm.

NUTRITIONAL INFORMATION

Per serving: 420 calories, 20g protein, 8g carbohydrates, 36g fat, 3g fiber, 120mg cholesterol, 500mg sodium, 200mg potassium.

Crockpot Low-Carb Meatballs

INGREDIENTS

- 2 lbs ground beef (or a mix of beef and pork)
- 1/2 cup almond flour
- 1/4 cup grated Parmesan cheese
- 1 egg, beaten
- 2 cloves garlic, minced
- 1 teaspoon salt
- 1/2 teaspoon black pepper
- 1 teaspoon dried oregano
- 1 teaspoon dried basil
- 1/2 cup sugar-free marinara sauce (plus extra for serving)
- 1/4 cup water

Prep Time: 20 min

Cook Time: 4 hours

Serves: 6

DIRECTIONS

In a large bowl, combine the ground meat, almond flour, Parmesan cheese, beaten egg, minced garlic, salt, pepper, oregano, and basil. Mix well until the ingredients are evenly distributed. Form the mixture into meatballs, each about the size of a golf ball. Place the meatballs in the slow cooker. Pour the sugar-free marinara sauce and water over the meatballs. Gently stir to ensure all meatballs are coated with the sauce. Cover and cook on low for 4 hours, or until the meatballs are cooked through. Serve the meatballs with additional marinara sauce if desired.

NUTRITIONAL INFORMATION

Per serving: 350 calories, 28g protein, 4g carbohydrates, 24g fat, 2g fiber, 120mg cholesterol, 700mg sodium, 300mg potassium.

Slow Cooker Stuffed Jalapeños

INGREDIENTS

- 12 large jalapeños, halved lengthwise and seeds removed
- 8 oz cream cheese, softened
- 1 cup shredded cheddar cheese
- 1/2 pound ground sausage, cooked and crumbled
- 1/4 teaspoon garlic powder
- 1/4 teaspoon onion powder
- Salt and pepper to taste
- 1/4 cup water (for the slow cooker)

Prep Time: 20 min

Cook Time: 2 hours

Serves: 4

DIRECTIONS

In a bowl, mix together the softened cream cheese, shredded cheddar cheese, cooked sausage, garlic powder, onion powder, salt, and pepper until well combined. Stuff each jalapeño half with the cheese and sausage mixture, pressing firmly to fill. Pour 1/4 cup of water into the bottom of the slow cooker to create a moist cooking environment. Carefully place the stuffed jalapeños in the slow cooker, filling side up. You may stack them lightly if necessary. Cover and cook on high for 2 hours, or until the jalapeños are tender and the filling is hot. Serve warm as a delicious keto-friendly appetizer or snack.

NUTRITIONAL INFORMATION

Per serving: 300 calories, 18g protein, 6g carbohydrates, 24g fat, 1g fiber, 100mg cholesterol, 500mg sodium, 250mg potassium.

Crockpot BBQ Chicken Wings

INGREDIENTS

- 2 lbs chicken wings, tips removed and wings cut at the joints
- Salt and pepper to taste
- 1 cup keto-friendly BBQ sauce (sugar-free)
- 2 tablespoons apple cider vinegar
- 1 tablespoon olive oil
- 1 teaspoon smoked paprika
- 1/2 teaspoon garlic powder
- 1/2 teaspoon onion powder

Prep Time: 15 min

Cook Time: 3 hours

Serves: 4

DIRECTIONS

Season the chicken wings with salt and pepper. Place them in the slow cooker.

In a bowl, mix together the keto-friendly BBQ sauce, apple cider vinegar, olive oil, smoked paprika, garlic powder, and onion powder. Pour this mixture over the chicken wings in the slow cooker, ensuring they are well coated. Cover and cook on high for 3 hours, or until the wings are cooked through and tender. For a crispy finish, place the cooked wings on a baking sheet lined with foil and broil in the oven for 3-5 minutes on each side, or until they are crispy and slightly charred. Serve the wings hot, with extra BBQ sauce for dipping if desired.

NUTRITIONAL INFORMATION

Per serving: 320 calories, 24g protein, 5g carbohydrates, 22g fat, 1g fiber, 85mg cholesterol, 650mg sodium, 300mg potassium.

Slow Cooker Parmesan Ranch Mushrooms

INGREDIENTS

- 1 lb whole button mushrooms, cleaned
- 1/2 cup unsalted butter, melted
- 1 packet ranch dressing mix (ensure it's keto-friendly)
- 1/2 cup grated Parmesan cheese
- 1 teaspoon garlic powder
- Salt and pepper to taste
- Fresh parsley, chopped for garnish

Prep Time: 10 min

Cook Time: 3 hours

Serves: 4

DIRECTIONS

Place the cleaned mushrooms in the slow cooker. In a bowl, mix together the melted butter, ranch dressing mix, grated Parmesan cheese, and garlic powder. Season with salt and pepper to taste. Pour the Parmesan ranch mixture over the mushrooms in the slow cooker, stirring gently to ensure all mushrooms are well coated. Cover and cook on low for 3 hours, or until the mushrooms are tender and flavorful. Garnish with fresh parsley before serving.

NUTRITIONAL INFORMATION

Per serving: 250 calories, 6g protein, 4g carbohydrates, 24g fat, 1g fiber, 60mg cholesterol, 750mg sodium, 300mg potassium.

Crockpot Garlic Butter Shrimp

INGREDIENTS

- 2 lbs large shrimp, peeled and deveined
- 1/2 cup unsalted butter
- 4 cloves garlic, minced
- 1 lemon, juiced and zested
- 1 teaspoon paprika
- Salt and pepper to taste
- Fresh parsley, chopped for garnish

Prep Time: 10 min

Cook Time: 1.5 hours

Serves: 4

DIRECTIONS

Place the shrimp in the slow cooker. In a small saucepan, melt the butter over medium heat. Add the minced garlic and cook for 1-2 minutes until fragrant. Stir in the lemon juice, lemon zest, and paprika. Season with salt and pepper.
Pour the garlic butter mixture over the shrimp in the slow cooker. Stir gently to ensure the shrimp are evenly coated. Cover and cook on low for 1.5 hours, or just until the shrimp are pink and opaque. Garnish with fresh parsley before serving. Serve hot.

NUTRITIONAL INFORMATION

Per serving: 330 calories, 48g protein, 2g carbohydrates, 14g fat, 0g fiber, 365mg cholesterol, 300mg sodium, 300mg potassium.

Slow Cooker Smoked Paprika Almonds

INGREDIENTS

- 3 cups raw almonds
- 2 tablespoons olive oil
- 1 tablespoon smoked paprika
- 1 teaspoon garlic powder
- 1/2 teaspoon cayenne pepper (adjust to taste)
- 1 teaspoon sea salt

Prep Time: 5 min

Cook Time: 2 hours

Serves: 6

DIRECTIONS

In a large bowl, toss the almonds with the olive oil until they are well coated.

Add the smoked paprika, garlic powder, cayenne pepper, and sea salt to the almonds. Toss again until the almonds are evenly coated with the spices. Transfer the seasoned almonds to the slow cooker. Spread them out to form an even layer. Cover and cook on low for 2 hours, stirring every 30 minutes to ensure even cooking. Once done, spread the almonds out on a baking sheet to cool. They will become crunchier as they cool.

NUTRITIONAL INFORMATION

Per serving: 320 calories, 12g protein, 10g carbohydrates, 28g fat, 6g fiber, 0mg cholesterol, 390mg sodium, 400mg potassium.

Seafood

Slow Cooker Lemon Herb Salmon

INGREDIENTS

- 4 salmon fillets (about 6 ounces each)
- Salt and pepper to taste
- 2 lemons, one sliced and one juiced
- 2 tablespoons olive oil
- 2 cloves garlic, minced
- 1 teaspoon dried dill
- 1 teaspoon dried thyme
- 1/4 cup fresh parsley, chopped

 Prep Time: 10 min

 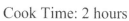 Cook Time: 2 hours

 Serves: 4

DIRECTIONS

Season the salmon fillets with salt and pepper. Place a layer of lemon slices at the bottom of the slow cooker. In a small bowl, whisk together the lemon juice, olive oil, minced garlic, dried dill, and dried thyme. Place the salmon fillets on top of the lemon slices in the slow cooker. Pour the lemon herb mixture over the salmon. Cover and cook on low for 2 hours, or until the salmon is cooked through and flakes easily with a fork. Garnish with fresh parsley before serving. Serve each fillet with a few of the cooked lemon slices.

NUTRITIONAL INFORMATION

Per serving: 280 calories, 34g protein, 3g carbohydrates, 15g fat, 1g fiber, 90mg cholesterol, 200mg sodium, 800mg potassium.

Keto Crockpot Shrimp Scampi

INGREDIENTS

- 2 lbs large shrimp, peeled and deveined
- 1/2 cup unsalted butter
- 1/4 cup olive oil
- 1/4 cup chicken broth
- 4 cloves garlic, minced
- 1 teaspoon red pepper flakes (adjust to taste)
- 1 lemon, juiced and zested
- Salt and pepper to taste
- 2 tablespoons fresh parsley, chopped
- 1/4 cup grated Parmesan cheese (optional)

 Prep Time: 10 min

 Cook Time: 2 hours

 Serves: 4

DIRECTIONS

Place the shrimp in the slow cooker. In a small saucepan, melt the butter with the olive oil over medium heat. Add the garlic and red pepper flakes, cooking for 1-2 minutes until fragrant but not browned. Stir in the chicken broth, lemon juice, and lemon zest. Season with salt and pepper. Pour the mixture over the shrimp in the slow cooker. Cover and cook on low for 1.5 to 2 hours, or just until the shrimp are pink and opaque. Stir in the fresh parsley and sprinkle with grated Parmesan cheese before serving, if using.

NUTRITIONAL INFORMATION

Per serving: 380 calories, 48g protein, 3g carbohydrates, 22g fat, 0g fiber, 340mg cholesterol, 300mg sodium, 300mg potassium.

Slow Cooker Coconut Curry Shrimp

INGREDIENTS

- 2 lbs large shrimp, peeled and deveined
- 1 can (14 oz) coconut milk
- 2 tablespoons curry powder
- 1 tablespoon tomato paste
- 1 red bell pepper, sliced
- 1 onion, chopped
- 3 cloves garlic, minced
- 1 tablespoon ginger, minced
- 1 teaspoon turmeric
- 1/2 teaspoon cayenne pepper (adjust to taste)
- Salt to taste
- 1 lime, juiced

Prep Time: 15 min

Cook Time: 3 hours

Serves: 4

DIRECTIONS

In the slow cooker, combine coconut milk, curry powder, tomato paste, red bell pepper, onion, garlic, ginger, turmeric, cayenne pepper, and salt. Stir well to combine. Add the shrimp to the slow cooker, stirring to ensure the shrimp are well coated with the curry mixture. Cover and cook on low for 3 hours, or until the shrimp are pink and cooked through. Stir in the lime juice just before serving. Garnish with fresh cilantro and serve hot.

NUTRITIONAL INFORMATION

Per serving: 330 calories, 38g protein, 10g carbohydrates, 16g fat, 2g fiber, 285mg cholesterol, 300mg sodium, 400mg potassium.

Crockpot Garlic Butter Lobster Tails

INGREDIENTS

- 4 lobster tails (5 to 6 ounces each), shell slit down the middle
- 1/2 cup unsalted butter, melted
- 4 cloves garlic, minced
- 1 teaspoon paprika
- Salt and pepper to taste
- Lemon wedges, for serving
- Fresh parsley, chopped for garnish

Prep Time: 10 min

Cook Time: 2 hours

Serves: 4

DIRECTIONS

Rinse the lobster tails and pat dry. With a pair of kitchen shears, carefully cut the top shell down the middle to expose the meat. In a small bowl, combine the melted butter, minced garlic, paprika, salt, and pepper. Place the lobster tails in the slow cooker, flesh side up. Spoon the garlic butter mixture over the lobster tails, making sure some of the mixture gets into the slit shells. Cover and cook on low for 2 hours, or until the lobster meat is opaque and cooked through. Serve the lobster tails immediately, garnished with fresh parsley and lemon wedges on the side.

NUTRITIONAL INFORMATION

Per serving: 230 calories, 24g protein, 1g carbohydrates, 14g fat, 0g fiber, 115mg cholesterol, 220mg sodium, 300mg potassium.

Slow Cooker Spicy Tuna Melt Pie

INGREDIENTS

For the crust:

- 1 cup almond flour
- 1/4 cup unsalted butter
- 1 egg
- 1/2 teaspoon salt

For the filling:

- 2 cans (5 ounces each) tuna, drained
- 1/2 cup mayonnaise
- 1/4 cup diced pickled jalapeños
- 1/2 cup diced red onion
- 1 teaspoon garlic powder
- 1/2 teaspoon smoked paprika
- 1 cup shredded cheddar cheese

 Prep Time: 20 min   Cook Time: 3 hours   Serves: 4

DIRECTIONS

In a bowl, mix almond flour, melted butter, egg, and salt until a dough forms. Press the dough into the bottom of a greased slow cooker to form a crust. In another bowl, combine tuna, mayonnaise, pickled jalapeños, red onion, garlic powder, smoked paprika, salt, and pepper. Mix well. Spread the tuna mixture evenly over the crust in the slow cooker. Top with shredded cheddar cheese.

Cover and cook on low for 3 hours, until the edges are golden and the cheese is melted and bubbly. Let cool for a few minutes before slicing. Serve warm.

NUTRITIONAL INFORMATION

Per serving: 480 calories, 28g protein, 8g carbohydrates, 38g fat, 3g fiber, 140mg cholesterol, 750mg sodium, 300mg potassium.

Crockpot Seafood Chowder

INGREDIENTS

- 1 lb mixed seafood
- 2 cups cauliflower florets, chopped
- 1 cup heavy cream
- 2 cups seafood or chicken broth
- 1/2 cup chopped celery
- 1/2 cup chopped onion
- 2 cloves garlic, minced
- 1 teaspoon dried thyme
- 1/2 teaspoon paprika
- Salt and pepper to taste
- 2 tablespoons butter

 Prep Time: 15 min   Cook Time: 6 hours   Serves: 4

DIRECTIONS

Place the cauliflower, celery, onion, garlic, thyme, paprika, salt, and pepper in the slow cooker. Pour in the broth and stir to combine. Cover and cook on low for 5 hours, until the vegetables are tender. Stir in the mixed seafood (shrimp, scallops, and lump crab meat), heavy cream, and butter. Cover and cook on high for 1 hour, or until the seafood is cooked through and the chowder is hot. Adjust seasoning with additional salt and pepper if needed. Serve hot, garnished with fresh parsley.

NUTRITIONAL INFORMATION

Per serving: 350 calories, 25g protein, 8g carbohydrates, 24g fat, 2g fiber, 180mg cholesterol, 600mg sodium, 400mg potassium.

Slow Cooker Cajun Shrimp and Sausage

INGREDIENTS

- 1 lb large shrimp, peeled and deveined
- 1 lb Andouille sausage, sliced
- 1 bell pepper, diced
- 1 onion, diced
- 2 stalks celery, diced
- 3 cloves garlic, minced
- 1 can (14.5 ounces) diced tomatoes, undrained
- 1 tablespoon Cajun seasoning
- 1/2 teaspoon smoked paprika

Prep Time: 15 min

Cook Time: 3 hours

Serves: 4

DIRECTIONS

Place the sliced sausage, diced bell pepper, onion, celery, and minced garlic in the slow cooker. Add the diced tomatoes with their juice. Sprinkle the Cajun seasoning and smoked paprika over the mixture. Season with salt and pepper to taste. Stir to combine all ingredients well. Cover and cook on low for 2.5 hours. Add the shrimp to the slow cooker, stirring gently to mix. Cover and cook on high for an additional 30 minutes, or until the shrimp are pink and cooked through. Serve hot, garnished with fresh parsley.

NUTRITIONAL INFORMATION

Per serving: 420 calories, 35g protein, 10g carbohydrates, 24g fat, 3g fiber, 220mg cholesterol, 1000mg sodium, 600mg potassium.

Crockpot Lemon Dill Cod

INGREDIENTS

- 4 cod fillets (about 6 ounces each)
- Salt and pepper to taste
- 2 tablespoons unsalted butter, melted
- Juice and zest of 1 lemon
- 2 cloves garlic, minced
- 1 tablespoon fresh dill, chopped (plus extra for garnish)
- 1/4 cup chicken broth or water

Prep Time: 10 min

Cook Time: 1.5-2 hours

Serves: 4

DIRECTIONS

Season the cod fillets with salt and pepper and place them in the slow cooker.

In a small bowl, mix together the melted butter, lemon juice and zest, minced garlic, and chopped dill. Pour this mixture over the cod fillets in the slow cooker. Add chicken broth or water to the bottom of the slow cooker to create a moist cooking environment and prevent the fish from drying out. Cover and cook on low for 1.5 to 2 hours, or until the cod is cooked through and flakes easily with a fork. Carefully remove the cod fillets from the slow cooker, garnish with additional fresh dill, and serve immediately.

NUTRITIONAL INFORMATION

Per serving: 160 calories, 26g protein, 1g carbohydrates, 5g fat, 0g fiber, 70mg cholesterol, 125mg sodium, 500mg potassium.

Slow Cooker Spicy Crab Dip

INGREDIENTS

- 1 lb lump crab meat, drained and picked over for shells
- 8 oz cream cheese
- 1 cup mayonnaise (preferably keto-friendly)
- 1/2 cup grated Parmesan cheese
- 3 green onions, chopped
- 2 cloves garlic, minced
- 1 jalapeño, seeded and finely chopped
- 1 tablespoon Worcestershire sauce
- 2 teaspoons hot sauce
- 1 teaspoon smoked paprika
- Salt and pepper to taste

 Prep Time: 10 min   Cook Time: 2 hours   Serves: 6

DIRECTIONS

In a large bowl, mix together the cream cheese, mayonnaise, grated Parmesan, green onions, minced garlic, chopped jalapeño, Worcestershire sauce, hot sauce, and smoked paprika until well combined. Season with salt and pepper to taste. Gently fold in the lump crab meat, being careful not to break up the lumps too much. Transfer the mixture to the slow cooker. Cover and cook on low for 2 hours, stirring gently once or twice during cooking if possible. Once hot and bubbly, give it a final gentle stir. Serve the crab dip warm with keto-friendly crackers, sliced cucumbers, or celery sticks for dipping.

NUTRITIONAL INFORMATION

Per serving: 360 calories, 24g protein, 2g carbohydrates, 28g fat, 0g fiber, 105mg cholesterol, 780mg sodium, 200mg potassium.

Crockpot Salmon with Creamy Herb Sauce

INGREDIENTS

- 4 salmon fillets (about 6 ounces each)
- Salt and pepper to taste
- 1 cup heavy cream
- 1 tablespoon Dijon mustard
- 2 tablespoons fresh dill, chopped
- 2 tablespoons fresh parsley, chopped
- 1 clove garlic, minced
- Juice of 1 lemon
- 1 tablespoon olive oil

 Prep Time: 10 min   Cook Time: 2 hours   Serves: 4

DIRECTIONS

Season the salmon fillets with salt and pepper. Place them in the slow cooker.

In a bowl, whisk together the heavy cream, Dijon mustard, dill, parsley, minced garlic, and lemon juice. Pour the creamy herb sauce over the salmon in the slow cooker. Drizzle with olive oil. Cover and cook on low for 2 hours, or until the salmon is cooked through and flakes easily with a fork. Carefully remove the salmon from the slow cooker and serve topped with the creamy herb sauce.

NUTRITIONAL INFORMATION

Per serving: 450 calories, 34g protein, 3g carbohydrates, 34g fat, 0g fiber, 140mg cholesterol, 300mg sodium, 700mg potassium.

Slow Cooker Garlic Parmesan Shrimp

INGREDIENTS

- 2 lbs large shrimp, peeled and deveined
- 1/2 cup unsalted butter
- 1/4 cup chicken broth
- 5 cloves garlic, minced
- 1/2 cup grated Parmesan cheese
- 1 teaspoon Italian seasoning
- Salt and pepper to taste
- Fresh parsley, chopped for garnish
- Lemon wedges, for serving

Prep Time: 10 min   Cook Time: 1 hour   Serves: 4 servings

DIRECTIONS

Place the shrimp in the slow cooker. In a saucepan, melt the butter over medium heat. Add the chicken broth and minced garlic, cooking for 1-2 minutes until the garlic is fragrant. Pour the garlic butter mixture over the shrimp in the slow cooker. Sprinkle with grated Parmesan cheese, Italian seasoning, salt, and pepper. Cover and cook on low for 1 hour, or until the shrimp are pink and cooked through. Avoid overcooking to prevent the shrimp from becoming tough. Garnish with fresh parsley and serve with lemon wedges on the side.

NUTRITIONAL INFORMATION

Per serving: 380 calories, 48g protein, 3g carbohydrates, 20g fat, 0g fiber, 330mg cholesterol, 460mg sodium, 350mg potassium.

Crockpot Clam and Vegetable Medley

INGREDIENTS

- 2 cans (6.5 ounces each) chopped clams, undrained
- 1 cup cauliflower florets, chopped
- 1 cup zucchini, diced
- 1/2 cup celery, diced
- 1/2 cup carrots, diced
- 1/2 cup onion, chopped
- 2 cloves garlic, minced
- 2 cups chicken or vegetable broth
- 1 teaspoon dried thyme
- 1 bay leaf
- 1/2 cup heavy cream

Prep Time: 15 min   Cook Time: 4 hours   Serves: 4

DIRECTIONS

In the slow cooker, combine the chopped clams with their juice, cauliflower, zucchini, celery, carrots (if using), onion, garlic, broth, thyme, and bay leaf. Season with salt and pepper to taste. Cover and cook on low for 4 hours, until vegetables are tender. Stir in the heavy cream and continue cooking on low for an additional 30 minutes. Remove the bay leaf before serving. Adjust seasoning if necessary. Garnish with fresh parsley and serve warm.

NUTRITIONAL INFORMATION

Per serving: 210 calories, 14g protein, 10g carbohydrates (7g without carrots), 12g fat, 2g fiber, 85mg cholesterol, 480mg sodium, 400mg potassium.

Slow Cooker Teriyaki Salmon and Vegetables

INGREDIENTS

- 4 salmon fillets (about 6 ounces each)
- 1 cup broccoli florets
- 1 cup snap peas
- 1 red bell pepper, sliced
- 1/2 cup keto-friendly teriyaki sauce (homemade or store-bought)
- 2 cloves garlic, minced
- 1 tablespoon ginger, grated
- Salt and pepper to taste
- Sesame seeds and sliced green onions for garnish

Prep Time: 15 min

Cook Time: 2 hours

Serves: 4

DIRECTIONS

In a small bowl, mix the keto-friendly teriyaki sauce with minced garlic and grated ginger. Season the salmon fillets with salt and pepper, and place them in the slow cooker. Surround the salmon with broccoli florets, snap peas, and sliced red bell pepper. Pour the teriyaki sauce mixture over the salmon and vegetables, ensuring everything is well coated. Cover and cook on low for 2 hours, or until the salmon is cooked through and the vegetables are tender.

Serve the teriyaki salmon and vegetables garnished with sesame seeds and sliced green onions.

NUTRITIONAL INFORMATION

Per serving: 320 calories, 35g protein, 8g carbohydrates, 16g fat, 2g fiber, 90mg cholesterol, 720mg sodium, 800mg potassium.

Crockpot Tomato Basil Scallops

INGREDIENTS

- 1.5 lbs sea scallops
- 1 can (14.5 ounces) diced tomatoes, drained
- 1/4 cup fresh basil, chopped
- 2 cloves garlic, minced
- 1/4 cup dry white wine (optional, can substitute with chicken broth for keto)
- 2 tablespoons olive oil
- Salt and pepper to taste
- Additional fresh basil for garnish

 Prep Time: 10 min

 Cook Time: 1.5 hour

 Serves: 4 servings

DIRECTIONS

Rinse the scallops and pat dry with paper towels. Season with salt and pepper.

In the slow cooker, combine the drained diced tomatoes, chopped basil, minced garlic, white wine (or chicken broth), and olive oil. Stir to mix well. Nestle the scallops into the tomato mixture in the slow cooker. Cover and cook on low for 1.5 hours, or until the scallops are tender and cooked through. Be careful not to overcook to prevent the scallops from becoming rubbery. Serve the scallops with the tomato basil sauce, garnished with additional fresh basil.

NUTRITIONAL INFORMATION

Per serving: 220 calories, 27g protein, 8g carbohydrates, 8g fat, 1g fiber, 56mg cholesterol, 700mg sodium, 500mg potassium.

Slow Cooker Spicy Shrimp Jambalaya

INGREDIENTS

- 1 lb large shrimp, peeled and deveined
- 1 lb Andouille sausage, sliced
- 1 cup cauliflower rice
- 1 bell pepper, diced
- 1 onion, diced
- 2 stalks celery, diced
- 3 cloves garlic, minced
- 1 can (14.5 ounces) diced tomatoes, undrained
- 1 cup chicken broth
- 2 teaspoons Cajun seasoning
- 1/2 teaspoon smoked paprika
- 1/4 teaspoon cayenne pepper (adjust to taste)
- Salt and pepper to taste
- 2 bay leaves
- Fresh parsley, chopped for garnish

 Prep Time: 15 min

 Cook Time: 5 hours

 Serves: 4 servings

DIRECTIONS

Place the sliced Andouille sausage, bell pepper, onion, celery, and minced garlic in the slow cooker. Add the diced tomatoes with their juice, chicken broth, Cajun seasoning, smoked paprika, cayenne pepper, salt, and pepper. Stir to combine. Submerge the bay leaves into the mixture. Cover and cook on low for 4.5 hours. Stir in the cauliflower rice and shrimp, and cook on high for an additional 30 minutes, or until the shrimp are pink and cooked through. Remove the bay leaves, and serve the jambalaya garnished with fresh parsley.

NUTRITIONAL INFORMATION

Per serving: 380 calories, 35g protein, 12g carbohydrates, 20g fat, 3g fiber, 220mg cholesterol, 1200mg sodium, 500mg potassium.

Poultry

Slow Cooker Chicken Alfredo

INGREDIENTS

- 4 boneless, skinless chicken breasts
- Salt and pepper to taste
- 1 tablespoon olive oil
- 1 cup heavy cream
- 1/2 cup chicken broth
- 2 cloves garlic, minced
- 1 cup grated Parmesan cheese
- 1/2 teaspoon garlic powder
- 1/2 teaspoon onion powder
- 1/2 teaspoon dried Italian seasoning
- Additional grated Parmesan and fresh parsley for garnish

Prep Time: 15 min

Cook Time: 4 hours

Serves: 4

DIRECTIONS

Season chicken with salt and pepper. Sear chicken in olive oil in a skillet over medium heat until golden (2-3 minutes per side). Transfer to slow cooker. In a bowl, whisk together heavy cream, chicken broth, minced garlic, grated Parmesan, garlic powder, onion powder, and Italian seasoning. Pour mixture over chicken in slow cooker. Cover and cook on low for 4 hours until chicken is cooked through. Remove chicken and set aside. If Alfredo sauce needs thickening, transfer to a saucepan and simmer to desired consistency. Serve chicken drizzled with Alfredo sauce, garnished with additional Parmesan and fresh parsley.

NUTRITIONAL INFORMATION

Per serving: 460 calories, 39g protein, 4g carbohydrates, 32g fat, 0g fiber, 155mg cholesterol, 620mg sodium, 300mg potassium.

Crockpot Buffalo Wings

INGREDIENTS

- 2 lbs chicken wings, tips removed and wings cut at the joints
- 1 cup buffalo wing sauce
- 2 tablespoons unsalted butter, melted
- 1 teaspoon garlic powder
- Salt and pepper to taste
- Blue cheese dressing for serving
- Celery sticks for serving

Prep Time: 10 min

Cook Time: 3 hours

Serves: 4 servings

DIRECTIONS

Season the chicken wings with salt, pepper, and garlic powder. Place them in the slow cooker. In a bowl, mix the buffalo wing sauce with the melted butter. Pour the mixture over the wings in the slow cooker, ensuring they are well coated. Cover and cook on high for 3 hours, or until the wings are cooked through. For a crispy finish, place the cooked wings on a baking sheet and broil in the oven for 3-5 minutes on each side. Serve the wings with blue cheese dressing and celery sticks on the side.

NUTRITIONAL INFORMATION

Per serving: 410 calories, 30g protein, 2g carbohydrates, 31g fat, 0g fiber, 115mg cholesterol, 1200mg sodium, 300mg potassium.

Keto Slow Cooker Chicken Marsala

INGREDIENTS

- 4 boneless, skinless chicken breasts
- Salt and pepper to taste
- 1 tablespoon olive oil
- 1/2 cup Marsala wine (choose a dry Marsala)
- 1 cup chicken broth, low sodium
- 8 ounces mushrooms, sliced
- 2 cloves garlic, minced
- 1/2 cup heavy cream
- 1 tablespoon arrowroot powder

 Prep Time: 15 min

 Cook Time: 4 hours

 Serves: 4

DIRECTIONS

Season the chicken breasts with salt and pepper. In a skillet over medium heat, heat the olive oil and brown the chicken on both sides for about 2-3 minutes per side. Transfer to the slow cooker. Add the sliced mushrooms and minced garlic over the chicken. Pour the Marsala wine and chicken broth into the slow cooker. Cover and cook on low for 4 hours, until the chicken is tender.

In the last 30 minutes of cooking, stir in the heavy cream. If you desire a thicker sauce, you can mix the arrowroot powder with a little water and stir it into the sauce. Serve the chicken and sauce garnished with chopped parsley.

NUTRITIONAL INFORMATION

Per serving: 310 calories, 25g protein, 7g carbohydrates, 18g fat, 1g fiber, 110mg cholesterol, 320mg sodium, 500mg potassium.

Slow Cooker Turkey and Avocado Chili

INGREDIENTS

- 1 lb ground turkey
- 1 large avocado, diced
- 1 can (14.5 ounces) diced tomatoes, undrained
- 1 can (4 ounces) diced green chilies
- 1 large onion, diced
- 2 cloves garlic, minced
- 1 tablespoon chili powder
- 1 teaspoon ground cumin
- 1/2 teaspoon smoked paprika
- Salt and pepper to taste
- 2 cups chicken broth
- Fresh cilantro, chopped for garnish

 Prep Time: 15 min

 Cook Time: 6 hours

 Serves: 4 servings

DIRECTIONS

In a skillet over medium heat, cook the ground turkey until browned. Drain any excess fat and transfer the turkey to the slow cooker. Add the diced avocado, diced tomatoes with their juice, green chilies, onion, garlic, chili powder, cumin, smoked paprika, salt, and pepper to the slow cooker with the turkey. Pour in the chicken broth and stir to combine all ingredients. Cover and cook on low for 6 hours, allowing the flavors to meld together. Serve the chili garnished with fresh cilantro. Optional: top with additional diced avocado or a dollop of sour cream if desired.

NUTRITIONAL INFORMATION

Per serving: 290 calories, 23g protein, 12g carbohydrates, 17g fat, 6g fiber, 60mg cholesterol, 570mg sodium, 800mg potassium.

Crockpot Chicken Parmesan

INGREDIENTS

- 4 boneless, skinless chicken breasts
- Salt and pepper to taste
- 1 cup keto-friendly marinara sauce
- 1 cup shredded mozzarella cheese
- 1/2 cup grated Parmesan cheese
- 1 teaspoon Italian seasoning
- 2 cloves garlic, minced
- 1/4 cup almond flour
- 2 tablespoons olive oil
- Fresh basil, chopped for garnish

Prep Time: 15 min

Cook Time: 4 hours

Serves: 4

DIRECTIONS

Season the chicken breasts with salt and pepper, then dredge in almond flour. In a skillet, heat the olive oil over medium heat. Add the chicken and sear until golden brown on both sides, about 3-4 minutes per side. Transfer to the slow cooker. Pour the marinara sauce over the chicken. Sprinkle minced garlic, Italian seasoning, shredded mozzarella, and grated Parmesan cheese on top.

Cover and cook on low for 4 hours, until the chicken is cooked through and the cheese is melted and bubbly. Serve garnished with fresh basil. Optional: Serve over zucchini noodles or cauliflower rice for a complete keto meal.

NUTRITIONAL INFORMATION

Per serving: 350 calories, 38g protein, 6g carbohydrates, 20g fat, 2g fiber, 105mg cholesterol, 680mg sodium, 400mg potassium.

Slow Cooker Moroccan Chicken

INGREDIENTS

- 4 boneless, skinless chicken breasts
- 1 large onion, chopped
- 2 cloves garlic, minced
- 1 teaspoon ground cumin, cinnamon, ginger
- 1/2 teaspoon ground turmeric
- 1/2 teaspoon cayenne pepper (adjust to taste)
- 1 can (14.5 ounces) diced tomatoes, undrained
- 1/2 cup chicken broth
- 1/4 cup chopped dried apricots
- 1/4 cup sliced almonds, toasted

Prep Time: 20 min

Cook Time: 6 hours

Serves: 4

DIRECTIONS

Season the chicken breasts with salt, pepper, cumin, cinnamon, ginger, turmeric, and cayenne pepper. Place them in the slow cooker. Add the chopped onion, minced garlic, diced tomatoes with their juice, and chicken broth to the slow cooker. If using, add the chopped dried apricots. Cover and cook on low for 6 hours, until the chicken is tender and the flavors have melded together. Serve the Moroccan chicken garnished with toasted sliced almonds and fresh cilantro.

NUTRITIONAL INFORMATION

Per serving: 270 calories, 35g protein, 8g carbohydrates, 10g fat, 2g fiber, 85mg cholesterol, 320mg sodium, 600mg potassium.

Crockpot Salsa Verde Chicken

INGREDIENTS

- 4 boneless, skinless chicken breasts
- 1 jar (16 ounces) salsa verde (check for no added sugars to keep it keto-friendly)
- 1 onion, chopped
- 2 cloves garlic, minced
- 1 teaspoon ground cumin
- Salt and pepper to taste
- Fresh cilantro, chopped for garnish
- 1 lime, cut into wedges for serving

 Prep Time: 5 min

 Cook Time: 4 hours

 Serves: 4

DIRECTIONS

Place the chicken breasts in the slow cooker. Season them with salt, pepper, and ground cumin. Add the chopped onion and minced garlic over the chicken. Pour the salsa verde evenly over everything. Cover and cook on low for 4 hours, until the chicken is tender and easily shreds with a fork. Shred the chicken with two forks inside the slow cooker, mixing it well with the salsa verde sauce. Serve hot, garnished with fresh cilantro and lime wedges on the side.

NUTRITIONAL INFORMATION

Per serving: 220 calories, 26g protein, 6g carbohydrates, 10g fat, 1g fiber, 65mg cholesterol, 690mg sodium, 400mg potassium.

Slow Cooker Chicken Cacciatore

INGREDIENTS

- 4 boneless, skinless chicken breasts
- Salt and pepper to taste
- 1 tablespoon olive oil
- 1 onion, sliced
- 2 bell peppers, sliced
- 3 cloves garlic, minced
- 1 can (14.5 ounces) diced tomatoes, no sugar added
- 1/2 cup chicken broth, low sodium
- 1 teaspoon dried oregano
- 1 teaspoon dried basil
- 1/2 teaspoon red pepper flakes (optional)
- 1/4 cup grated Parmesan cheese (for serving)

 Prep Time: 20 min

Cook Time: 6 hour

 Serves: 4 servings

DIRECTIONS

Season the chicken breasts with salt and pepper. In a skillet over medium-high heat, heat the olive oil and brown the chicken on both sides. Transfer to the slow cooker. In the same skillet, sauté the onion, bell peppers, and garlic for 2-3 minutes until slightly softened. Transfer to the slow cooker over the chicken. Add the diced tomatoes, chicken broth, oregano, basil, and red pepper flakes to the slow cooker. Stir gently to combine. Cover and cook on low for 6 hours, until the chicken is tender. Serve the chicken cacciatore garnished with fresh basil or parsley and sprinkled with grated Parmesan cheese.

NUTRITIONAL INFORMATION

Per serving: 260 calories, 30g protein, 10g carbohydrates, 10g fat, 3g fiber, 75mg cholesterol, 420mg sodium, 700mg potassium.

Crockpot BBQ Chicken Thighs

INGREDIENTS

- 8 chicken thighs, bone-in and skin-on
- Salt and pepper to taste
- 1 cup keto-friendly BBQ sauce (sugar-free)
- 2 tablespoons apple cider vinegar
- 1 tablespoon smoked paprika
- 1 teaspoon garlic powder
- 1/2 teaspoon onion powder
- Optional: fresh parsley or cilantro for garnish

Prep Time: 10 min   Cook Time: 4 hours   Serves: 4

DIRECTIONS

Season the chicken thighs with salt and pepper. Place them in the slow cooker. In a bowl, mix together the keto-friendly BBQ sauce, apple cider vinegar, smoked paprika, garlic powder, and onion powder. Pour this mixture over the chicken thighs in the slow cooker, ensuring each thigh is well coated.

Cover and cook on low for 4 hours, or until the chicken is tender and fully cooked. For a crispy skin, transfer the cooked chicken thighs to a baking sheet and broil in the oven for 3-5 minutes, or until the skin is crispy. Serve hot, garnished with fresh parsley or cilantro if desired.

NUTRITIONAL INFORMATION

Per serving: 320 calories, 35g protein, 5g carbohydrates, 18g fat, 1g fiber, 185mg cholesterol, 590mg sodium, 400mg potassium.

Slow Cooker Lemon Herb Roast Chicken

INGREDIENTS

- 1 whole chicken (about 4 to 5 pounds), giblets removed
- Salt and pepper to taste
- 2 tablespoons olive oil
- 1 lemon, halved
- 4 cloves garlic, minced
- 2 tablespoons fresh rosemary, chopped
- 2 tablespoons fresh thyme, chopped
- 1 tablespoon dried oregano
- 1/2 cup chicken broth

Prep Time: 20 minutes

Cook Time: **4-7** hours

Serves: 6

DIRECTIONS

Season inside and outside of chicken with salt and pepper. Place lemon halves, half of minced garlic, rosemary, and thyme inside the cavity. In a small bowl, mix olive oil, remaining garlic, rosemary, thyme, and oregano. Rub this mixture over the chicken. Pour chicken broth into the slow cooker. Place seasoned chicken breast side up in the slow cooker. Cover and cook on high for 4 hours or low for 7 hours, until the chicken reaches 165°F internal temperature. For crispy skin, transfer cooked chicken to a broiler pan and broil for 3-5 minutes until golden. Let chicken rest for 10 minutes before carving. Serve with slow cooker juices.

NUTRITIONAL INFORMATION

Per serving: 370 calories, 35g protein, 1g carbohydrates, 25g fat, 0g fiber, 105mg cholesterol, 620mg sodium, 350mg potassium.

Crockpot Chicken and Mushroom Gravy

INGREDIENTS

- 4 boneless, skinless chicken breasts
- Salt and pepper to taste
- 1 tablespoon olive oil
- 2 cups sliced mushrooms
- 1 clove garlic, minced
- 1 cup chicken broth, low sodium
- 1/2 cup heavy cream
- 2 tablespoons unsalted butter
- 1 teaspoon xanthan gum (for thickening, optional)
- Fresh thyme for garnish

 Prep Time: 15 min

 Cook Time: 6 hours

 Serves: 4

DIRECTIONS

Season chicken breasts with salt and pepper. Brown chicken on both sides in olive oil in a skillet over medium heat. Transfer to slow cooker. Add sliced mushrooms, minced garlic, and chicken broth to slow cooker. Cover and cook on low for 5-6 hours until chicken is tender. Remove chicken. Turn slow cooker to high. Stir in heavy cream and butter. If using xanthan gum, sprinkle it in now, whisking vigorously to avoid clumps. Return chicken to slow cooker, coating it in the gravy. Cover and cook on high for 15-20 minutes until gravy is thickened and heated through. Serve chicken and mushroom gravy garnished with fresh thyme.

NUTRITIONAL INFORMATION

Per serving: 310 calories, 29g protein, 4g carbohydrates, 20g fat, 1g fiber, 120mg cholesterol, 320mg sodium, 450mg potassium.

Slow Cooker Teriyaki Chicken

INGREDIENTS

- 4 boneless, skinless chicken breasts
- 1/2 cup keto-friendly teriyaki sauce (look for or make a sugar-free version)
- 1/4 cup water
- 2 cloves garlic, minced
- 1 tablespoon fresh ginger, grated
- 1 tablespoon sesame oil
- 1 tablespoon apple cider vinegar
- 1 teaspoon xanthan gum (optional, for thickening)
- Sesame seeds and sliced green onions for garnish

 Prep Time: 10 min

 Cook Time: 4 hours

 Serves: 4

DIRECTIONS

Place the chicken breasts in the slow cooker. In a bowl, whisk together the keto-friendly teriyaki sauce, water, minced garlic, grated ginger, sesame oil, and apple cider vinegar. Pour this mixture over the chicken in the slow cooker.

Cover and cook on low for 4 hours, until the chicken is cooked through and tender. If you prefer a thicker sauce, mix the xanthan gum with a little bit of the sauce from the slow cooker in a separate bowl until smooth. Stir this mixture back into the slow cooker, and cook on high for an additional 15-20 minutes, or until the sauce has thickened. Serve the teriyaki chicken garnished with sesame seeds and sliced green onions.

NUTRITIONAL INFORMATION

Per serving: 230 calories, 27g protein, 3g carbohydrates, 12g fat, 0g fiber, 75mg cholesterol, 500mg sodium, 300mg potassium.

Crockpot Spinach and Feta Chicken

INGREDIENTS

- 4 boneless, skinless chicken breasts
- Salt and pepper to taste
- 2 cups fresh spinach, roughly chopped
- 1 cup feta cheese, crumbled
- 1/4 cup sun-dried tomatoes, chopped (optional, check for added sugars)
- 2 cloves garlic, minced
- 1 tablespoon olive oil
- 1/2 teaspoon dried oregano
- 1/4 cup chicken broth

 Prep Time: 15 min

 Cook Time: 4 hours

 Serves: 4

DIRECTIONS

Season the chicken breasts with salt and pepper. Lay them flat in the slow cooker. In a bowl, mix together the chopped spinach, crumbled feta cheese, sun-dried tomatoes (if using), minced garlic, olive oil, and dried oregano. Spread the spinach and feta mixture over the chicken breasts in the slow cooker. Pour the chicken broth around the chicken breasts. The broth will help keep the chicken moist during cooking. Cover and cook on low for 4 hours, or until the chicken is cooked through and tender. Serve the chicken breasts with the creamy spinach and feta topping.

NUTRITIONAL INFORMATION

Per serving: 280 calories, 35g protein, 4g carbohydrates, 14g fat, 1g fiber, 105mg cholesterol, 620mg sodium, 500mg potassium.

Slow Cooker Chicken Tikka Masala

INGREDIENTS

- 2 lbs boneless, skinless chicken thighs, cut into bite-sized pieces
- 1 onion, finely chopped
- 3 cloves garlic, minced
- 1 tablespoon fresh ginger, grated
- 1 can (14 oz) diced tomatoes, no sugar added
- 1/4 cup coconut cream
- 2 tablespoons tomato paste
- 2 tablespoons garam masala
- 1 teaspoon turmeric, cumin
- 1/2 teaspoon chili powder
- 1/2 cup chicken broth

Prep Time: 20 min   Cook Time: 6 hours   Serves: 4

DIRECTIONS

Season the chicken pieces with salt and pepper and place them in the slow cooker. Add the chopped onion, minced garlic, grated ginger, diced tomatoes, coconut cream, tomato paste, garam masala, turmeric, cumin, and chili powder to the slow cooker. Stir to combine everything well. Pour the chicken broth over the mixture, ensuring the chicken is well-coated with the spices and liquids. Cover and cook on low for 6 hours, or until the chicken is tender and the sauce is flavorful. Before serving, stir the sauce well and adjust seasoning if needed. Serve the chicken tikka masala over cauliflower rice, garnished with fresh cilantro.

NUTRITIONAL INFORMATION

Per serving: 350 calories, 43g protein, 8g carbohydrates, 16g fat, 2g fiber, 180mg cholesterol, 400mg sodium, 700mg potassium.

Crockpot Greek Lemon Chicken Soup

INGREDIENTS

- 4 cups chicken broth, low sodium
- 2 boneless, skinless chicken breasts
- 1 onion, chopped
- 2 cloves garlic, minced
- 1/2 cup celery, chopped
- 1/2 cup carrots, chopped (optional, omit for stricter keto)
- 1/3 cup fresh lemon juice
- 2 teaspoons dried oregano
- Salt and pepper to taste
- 2 large eggs
- 1/4 cup fresh dill, chopped
- Additional lemon slices for garnish

Prep Time: 15 min

Cook Time: 6 hours

Serves: 4

DIRECTIONS

In the slow cooker, combine the chicken broth, chicken breasts, onion, garlic, celery, carrots (if using), lemon juice, oregano, salt, and pepper. Cover and cook on low for 6 hours, or until the chicken is tender and fully cooked. Remove the chicken from the slow cooker, shred it with two forks, and return it to the pot. In a medium bowl, whisk the eggs until frothy. Slowly ladle some of the hot soup into the eggs, whisking constantly to temper them. Then, slowly stir the egg mixture back into the slow cooker to thicken the soup. Add the chopped dill and adjust seasoning if needed. Cook on low for an additional 15 minutes to heat through. Serve the soup hot, garnished with lemon slices.

NUTRITIONAL INFORMATION

Per serving: 200 calories, 25g protein, 6g carbohydrates (4g without carrots), 8g fat, 1g fiber, 140mg cholesterol, 300mg sodium, 500mg potassium.

Meat

Slow Cooker Keto Beef Stroganoff

INGREDIENTS

- 2 lbs beef chuck roast, cut into 1-inch cubes
- Salt and pepper to taste
- 1 tablespoon olive oil
- 1 onion, thinly sliced
- 2 cloves garlic, minced
- 8 ounces mushrooms, sliced
- 1 cup beef broth, low sodium
- 1 tablespoon Worcestershire sauce (check for a keto-friendly version)
- 1 teaspoon Dijon mustard
- 1 cup sour cream

 Prep Time: 15 min

 Cook Time: 8 hours

 Serves: 4

DIRECTIONS

Season beef cubes, brown in olive oil, transfer to slow cooker. Sauté onion and garlic in the skillet, add mushrooms and cook until browned. Transfer vegetables to slow cooker. Pour beef broth over, stir in Worcestershire sauce and Dijon mustard. Cook on low for 8 hours. Stir in sour cream just before serving, adjust seasoning. Serve garnished with parsley. For a keto meal, serve over cauliflower rice or zucchini noodles.

NUTRITIONAL INFORMATION

Per serving: 540 calories, 48g protein, 8g carbohydrates, 36g fat, 1g fiber, 155mg cholesterol, 390mg sodium, 800mg potassium.

Crockpot Pulled Pork with Keto BBQ Sauce

INGREDIENTS

- 3 lbs pork shoulder
- 1 tablespoon smoked paprika, garlic powder, onion powder
- 1/2 cup apple cider vinegar
- 1 cup water

For the Keto BBQ Sauce:

- 1 cup sugar-free tomato sauce
- 2 tablespoons apple cider vinegar, Worcestershire sauce
- 1 tablespoon liquid smoke, smoked paprika
- 1 teaspoon garlic powder, onion powder
- Sweetener equivalent to 2 tablespoons sugar

 Prep Time: 15 min

 Cook Time: 8 hours

 Serves: 6

DIRECTIONS

Rub pork shoulder with salt, pepper, smoked paprika, garlic powder, and onion powder. Place in slow cooker. Add apple cider vinegar and water. Cook on low for 8 hours until pork is tender and shreds easily. 30 minutes before done, mix all BBQ sauce ingredients in a saucepan, simmer for 20 minutes. Remove pork, shred, discard excess fat. Drain cooking liquid, leaving some to moisten pork. Return shredded pork to slow cooker, mix in BBQ sauce. Cook on low for an additional 30 minutes. Serve with extra BBQ sauce on the side if desired.

NUTRITIONAL INFORMATION

Per serving: 320 calories, 38g protein, 3g carbohydrates, 18g fat, 1g fiber, 105mg cholesterol, 390mg sodium, 700mg potassium.

Slow Cooker Lamb Curry

INGREDIENTS

- 2 lbs lamb shoulder, cut into 1-inch cubes
- 1 large onion, chopped
- 3 cloves garlic, minced
- 1 tablespoon fresh ginger, grated
- 2 tablespoons curry powder
- 1 teaspoon ground turmeric
- 1 teaspoon ground cumin
- 1/2 teaspoon cayenne pepper (adjust to taste)
- 1 can (14 oz) diced tomatoes, no sugar added
- 1 cup coconut milk
- 1/2 cup fresh cilantro, chopped for garnish

Prep Time: 20 min

Cook Time: 8 hours

Serves: 6

DIRECTIONS

Season the lamb cubes with salt and pepper. In a skillet over medium-high heat, heat the olive oil and brown the lamb on all sides. Transfer to the slow cooker. In the same skillet, add the onion, garlic, and ginger, sautéing until softened. Stir in the curry powder, turmeric, cumin, and cayenne pepper, cooking for another minute until fragrant. Add to the slow cooker. Pour the diced tomatoes and their juice over the lamb. Stir in the coconut milk until everything is well combined. Cover and cook on low for 8 hours, or until the lamb is tender and the flavors are melded. Serve the lamb curry garnished with fresh cilantro. For a complete keto meal, serve over cauliflower rice.

NUTRITIONAL INFORMATION

Per serving: 380 calories, 35g protein, 8g carbohydrates, 24g fat, 2g fiber, 105mg cholesterol, 320mg sodium, 600mg potassium.

Keto Meatball Sub Casserole in a Crockpot

INGREDIENTS

For the Meatballs:

- 1.5 lbs ground beef
- 1/4 cup almond flour, grated Parmesan cheese
- 1 egg
- 2 cloves garlic, minced
- 1 teaspoon salt
- 1/2 teaspoon black pepper
- 1 teaspoon Italian seasoning

For the Casserole:

- 2 cups marinara sauce
- 2 cups shredded mozzarella cheese
- 1/2 cup grated Parmesan cheese

Prep Time: 20 min

Cook Time: 4 hours

Serves: 6

DIRECTIONS

Mix the ground beef, almond flour, grated Parmesan, egg, minced garlic, salt, pepper, and Italian seasoning in a bowl. Form into meatballs, approximately 1 inch in diameter. Grease the inside of the crockpot with olive oil. Place the meatballs in the crockpot. Pour the marinara sauce over the meatballs. Cover and cook on low for 4 hours, or until the meatballs are cooked through. Sprinkle the shredded mozzarella and grated Parmesan cheese over the meatballs. Cover again and cook for an additional 30 minutes, or until the cheese is melted and bubbly. Garnish with additional Italian seasoning before serving.

NUTRITIONAL INFORMATION

Per serving: 450 calories, 35g protein, 6g carbohydrates, 34g fat, 2g fiber, 140mg cholesterol, 720mg sodium, 500mg potassium.

Slow Cooker Bacon-Wrapped Pork Loin

INGREDIENTS

- 1 pork loin (about 2-3 lbs)
- Salt and pepper to taste
- 2 teaspoons garlic powder
- 2 teaspoons smoked paprika
- 10-12 slices of bacon
- 1/4 cup olive oil
- 1/2 cup chicken broth, low sodium
- 2 tablespoons Dijon mustard
- 2 cloves garlic, minced
- Fresh herbs (rosemary or thyme) for garnish

 Prep Time: 20 min

  Cook Time: 6 hours

 Serves: 6

DIRECTIONS

Season pork loin with salt, pepper, garlic powder, and smoked paprika. Wrap with bacon slices, covering the surface. Whisk together olive oil, chicken broth, Dijon mustard, and minced garlic. Pour into slow cooker. Place bacon-wrapped pork loin in the slow cooker, ensuring the liquid doesn't cover it. Cook on low for 6 hours or until pork reaches 145°F. Remove, let it rest for 10 minutes, then slice. Garnish with fresh herbs. Broil for 2-3 minutes to crisp up bacon before serving.

NUTRITIONAL INFORMATION

Per serving: 450 calories, 35g protein, 0g carbohydrates, 35g fat, 0g fiber, 105mg cholesterol, 590mg sodium, 500mg potassium.

Crockpot Beef Bourguignon

INGREDIENTS

- 2 pounds beef chuck, cut into 1-inch cubes
- 1/4 cup almond flour for dredging
- 2 tablespoons olive oil
- 1/2 cup low-sodium beef broth
- 1/2 cup dry red wine
- 1 medium onion, chopped
- 4 cloves garlic, minced
- 8 ounces mushrooms, sliced
- 2 medium carrots, sliced
- 1 tablespoon tomato paste
- 2 teaspoons fresh thyme, or 1 teaspoon dried thyme
- 2 bay leaves

 Prep Time: 20 minutes

 Cook Time: 8 hours

 Serves: 4

DIRECTIONS

Toss the beef cubes with almond flour, salt, and pepper. Heat olive oil in a skillet over medium-high heat. Add the beef and cook until browned on all sides. Transfer to the slow cooker. In the same skillet, add a bit more oil if needed, and sauté the onion and garlic until soft. Add mushrooms and cook for another 5 minutes. Transfer the mixture to the slow cooker. Add beef broth, red wine, tomato paste, thyme, bay leaves, and carrots (if using) to the slow cooker. Stir to combine. Cover and cook on low for 8 hours or until the beef is tender. Remove bay leaves before serving. Adjust seasoning with salt and pepper to taste.

NUTRITIONAL INFORMATION

Per serving: 450 calories, 35g protein, 10g carbohydrates, 25g fat, 2g fiber, 100mg cholesterol, 200mg sodium, 750mg potassium.

Slow Cooker Pork Chops and Gravy

INGREDIENTS

- 4 bone-in pork chops, about 1 inch thick
- Salt and pepper to taste
- 1 tablespoon olive oil
- 1 cup chicken broth, low sodium
- 1/2 cup sour cream
- 2 tablespoons Dijon mustard
- 2 cloves garlic, minced
- 1 teaspoon dried thyme
- 2 tablespoons almond flour (for thickening)
- Fresh parsley, chopped for garnish

 Prep Time: 10 min

 Cook Time: 6 hours

 Serves: 4

DIRECTIONS

Season pork chops with salt and pepper. Brown in olive oil in a skillet over medium-high heat, about 3-4 minutes per side. Transfer to slow cooker. Whisk together chicken broth, sour cream, Dijon mustard, minced garlic, and dried thyme. Pour over pork chops in slow cooker. Cover and cook on low for 6 hours until pork chops are tender. Remove pork chops. Stir almond flour into the gravy to thicken, adjust seasoning. If gravy is thin, cook on high in slow cooker with lid off for a few minutes to reduce. Serve pork chops with gravy poured over, garnished with fresh parsley.

NUTRITIONAL INFORMATION

Per serving: 300 calories, 29g protein, 3g carbohydrates, 20g fat, 1g fiber, 90mg cholesterol, 320mg sodium, 500mg potassium.

Crockpot Italian Beef Roast

INGREDIENTS

- 3 lbs beef roast (such as chuck roast)
- Salt and pepper to taste
- 1 tablespoon olive oil
- 4 cloves garlic, minced
- 1 tablespoon dried Italian seasoning
- 1/2 cup beef broth, low sodium
- 1/2 cup pepperoncini peppers, sliced
- 1/4 cup juice from pepperoncini jar
- 1 onion, sliced
- 2 bay leaves

Prep Time: 10 min   Cook Time: 8 hours   Serves: 6

DIRECTIONS

Season the beef roast with salt and pepper. In a skillet over medium-high heat, heat the olive oil and sear the roast on all sides until browned. Transfer to the slow cooker. Add the minced garlic, Italian seasoning, beef broth, pepperoncini peppers and juice, sliced onion, and bay leaves to the slow cooker. Stir to mix the ingredients around the roast. Cover and cook on low for 8 hours, or until the beef is tender and shreds easily with a fork. Remove the bay leaves and shred the beef with two forks in the slow cooker, mixing it with the juices and vegetables. Serve the Italian beef with its juices, ideal for a keto-friendly meal or wrapped in low-carb tortillas if desired.

NUTRITIONAL INFORMATION

Per serving: 400 calories, 45g protein, 3g carbohydrates, 24g fat, 1g fiber, 120mg cholesterol, 350mg sodium, 600mg potassium.

Slow Cooker Smoky Beef Brisket

INGREDIENTS

- 3 pounds beef brisket
- 2 tablespoons smoked paprika
- 1 tablespoon garlic powder
- 1 tablespoon onion powder
- 1 teaspoon cayenne pepper (adjust to taste)
- Salt and black pepper to taste
- 1/4 cup apple cider vinegar
- 1/2 cup beef broth (low sodium)
- 2 tablespoons Worcestershire sauce
- 1 tablespoon liquid smoke
- 2 tablespoons olive oil

Prep Time: 15 min   Cook Time: 8 hours   Serves: 6

DIRECTIONS

Mix smoked paprika, garlic powder, onion powder, cayenne pepper, salt, and black pepper in a small bowl. Rub this mixture over beef brisket. Heat olive oil in a large skillet over medium-high heat. Sear brisket on both sides until a crust forms, about 3-4 minutes per side. Transfer brisket to the slow cooker. In the same skillet, combine apple cider vinegar, beef broth, Worcestershire sauce, and liquid smoke. Bring to a simmer, scraping off browned bits. Pour mixture over brisket in the slow cooker. Cover and cook on low for 8 hours until brisket is tender. Remove brisket, let it rest for 10 minutes before slicing against the grain. Serve with cooking juices drizzled over the top.

NUTRITIONAL INFORMATION

Per serving: 480 calories, 60g protein, 4g carbohydrates, 24g fat, 1g fiber, 175mg cholesterol, 350mg sodium, 800mg potassium.

Crockpot Corned Beef and Cabbage

INGREDIENTS

- 3 pounds corned beef brisket (with spice packet)
- 4 cups water
- 2 tablespoons apple cider vinegar
- 2 tablespoons Worcestershire sauce
- 1 onion, quartered
- 3 garlic cloves, minced
- 1 teaspoon black peppercorns
- 2 bay leaves
- 1 small head of cabbage, cut into wedges
- 8 radishes, halved (as a low-carb potato substitute)

Prep Time: 10 min

Cook Time: 8 hours

Serves: 6

DIRECTIONS

Place the corned beef brisket in the slow cooker. Add the spice packet that comes with the corned beef, water, apple cider vinegar, Worcestershire sauce, onion, garlic, peppercorns, and bay leaves. Cover and cook on low for 7 hours. After 7 hours, add the cabbage wedges and radishes to the slow cooker. Cover and continue cooking on low for 1 more hour, or until the vegetables are tender and the meat easily pulls apart. Remove the bay leaves and slice the corned beef against the grain. Serve with the cooked vegetables and a spoonful of the cooking liquid.

NUTRITIONAL INFORMATION

Per serving: 450 calories, 35g protein, 8g carbohydrates, 32g fat, 3g fiber, 120mg cholesterol, 950mg sodium, 600mg potassium.

INGREDIENTS

- 2 lbs beef short ribs
- Salt and pepper to taste
- 1/4 cup soy sauce (or tamari for gluten-free)
- 2 tablespoons erythritol (or other keto-friendly sweetener)
- 4 cloves garlic, minced
- 1 inch fresh ginger, grated
- 2 tablespoons rice vinegar
- 1 tablespoon sesame oil
- 1 teaspoon red pepper flakes (adjust to taste)
- 4 green onions, chopped
- 1 tablespoon sesame seeds

Prep Time: 15 min   Cook Time: 8 hours   Serves: 4

DIRECTIONS

Season the beef short ribs with salt and pepper and place them in the slow cooker. In a bowl, whisk together soy sauce, erythritol, minced garlic, grated ginger, rice vinegar, sesame oil, and red pepper flakes. Pour this mixture over the ribs in the slow cooker. Cover and cook on low for 8 hours, or until the ribs are tender and falling off the bone. Carefully remove the ribs from the slow cooker. Skim off any excess fat from the surface of the cooking liquid. Serve the ribs garnished with chopped green onions and sesame seeds. For a complete keto meal, serve with cauliflower rice or steamed vegetables.

NUTRITIONAL INFORMATION

Per serving: 500 calories, 25g protein, 5g carbohydrates, 40g fat, 1g fiber, 120mg cholesterol, 700mg sodium, 350mg potassium.

Crockpot Spicy Pulled Beef

INGREDIENTS

- 3 lbs beef chuck roast
- Salt and pepper to taste
- 1 tablespoon smoked paprika
- 2 teaspoons cumin
- 1 teaspoon cayenne pepper (adjust to taste for spiciness)
- 4 cloves garlic, minced
- 1 large onion, sliced
- 1/2 cup beef broth, low sodium
- 1/4 cup apple cider vinegar
- 2 tablespoons sugar-free hot sauce
- 1 tablespoon Worcestershire sauce

Prep Time: 15 min

Cook Time: 8 hours

Serves: 6

DIRECTIONS

Season the beef chuck roast with salt, pepper, smoked paprika, cumin, and cayenne pepper. Place it in the crockpot. Add the minced garlic, sliced onion, beef broth, apple cider vinegar, hot sauce, and Worcestershire sauce over the beef. Cover and cook on low for 8 hours, or until the beef is tender and easily shreds with a fork. Remove the beef from the crockpot and shred with two forks. Return the shredded beef to the crockpot and mix with the juices and cooked onions. Serve the spicy pulled beef with additional hot sauce if desired. This dish pairs well with keto-friendly sides such as cauliflower mash or a green leafy salad.

NUTRITIONAL INFORMATION

Per serving: 380 calories, 35g protein, 3g carbohydrates, 26g fat, 1g fiber, 105mg cholesterol, 450mg sodium, 600mg potassium.

Slow Cooker Texas Chili

INGREDIENTS

- 2 lbs ground beef (80/20)
- 1 large onion, finely chopped
- 4 cloves garlic, minced
- 2 tablespoons chili powder
- 1 tablespoon cumin
- 1 tablespoon smoked paprika
- 2 teaspoons oregano
- 1 teaspoon cayenne pepper
- Salt and pepper to taste
- 1 can (6 oz) tomato paste
- 1 cup beef broth, low sodium
- 1/4 cup apple cider vinegar
- 2 bay leaves

Prep Time: 20 min

Cook Time: 8 hours

Serves: 6

DIRECTIONS

In a skillet over medium-high heat, brown the ground beef with the onion and garlic until the beef is no longer pink. Drain any excess fat. Transfer the beef mixture to the slow cooker. Add chili powder, cumin, smoked paprika, oregano, cayenne pepper, salt, and pepper. Stir well to combine. Stir in the tomato paste, beef broth, and apple cider vinegar until well mixed. Add bay leaves. Cover and cook on low for 8 hours, allowing the flavors to meld and the chili to thicken. Remove bay leaves before serving. Adjust seasoning if necessary.

NUTRITIONAL INFORMATION

Per serving: 350 calories, 25g protein, 6g carbohydrates, 25g fat, 2g fiber, 80mg cholesterol, 500mg sodium, 400mg potassium.

Crockpot Maple Mustard Pork Tenderloin

INGREDIENTS

- 2 pounds pork tenderloin
- Salt and pepper to taste
- 2 tablespoons olive oil
- 1/4 cup Dijon mustard
- 3 tablespoons sugar-free maple syrup
- 2 cloves garlic, minced
- 1 tablespoon apple cider vinegar
- 1/2 teaspoon smoked paprika
- 1/4 cup chicken broth (low sodium)

Prep Time: 15 min

Cook Time: 4 hours

Serves: 4

DIRECTIONS

Season pork tenderloin with salt and pepper. Brown in olive oil in a skillet over medium-high heat, about 2-3 minutes per side. Transfer to slow cooker. Whisk together Dijon mustard, sugar-free maple syrup, minced garlic, apple cider vinegar, and smoked paprika in a small bowl. Pour over pork in slow cooker. Pour chicken broth around the pork. Cover and cook on low for 4 hours or until pork is tender and reaches 145°F internal temperature. Let pork rest for 5 minutes before slicing. Serve with sauce from slow cooker drizzled over the top.

NUTRITIONAL INFORMATION

Per serving: 300 calories, 35g protein, 4g carbohydrates, 16g fat, 0g fiber, 90mg cholesterol, 400mg sodium, 650mg potassium.

Slow Cooker Ropa Vieja

INGREDIENTS

- 2 lbs flank steak
- Salt and pepper to taste
- 1 large onion, thinly sliced
- 1 red bell pepper, thinly sliced
- 1 green bell pepper, thinly sliced
- 4 cloves garlic, minced
- 1 teaspoon ground cumin
- 1 teaspoon dried oregano
- 1/2 teaspoon paprika
- 1 can (14 oz) diced tomatoes, no sugar added
- 1/4 cup beef broth, low sodium
- 2 tablespoons apple cider vinegar
- 1/4 cup green olives, sliced
- 2 tablespoons capers (optional)
- Fresh cilantro, for garnish

Prep Time: 15 min

Cook Time: **8 hours**

Serves: 6

DIRECTIONS

Season the flank steak with salt and pepper and place it in the slow cooker. Add the sliced onion, bell peppers, minced garlic, cumin, oregano, and paprika over the steak. Pour the diced tomatoes, beef broth, and apple cider vinegar into the slow cooker. Stir gently to combine the ingredients. Cover and cook on low for 8 hours, or until the steak is very tender and shreds easily with a fork. Shred the beef using two forks and stir in the sliced olives and capers if using. Cook on low for an additional 30 minutes to blend the flavors.

Serve garnished with fresh cilantro. For a keto-friendly meal, serve with cauliflower rice or over a bed of mixed greens.

NUTRITIONAL INFORMATION

Per serving: 300 calories, 35g protein, 8g carbohydrates, 15g fat, 2g fiber, 90mg cholesterol, 500mg sodium, 600mg potassium.

Vegetarian Dishes

Slow Cooker Creamy Mushroom Stroganoff

INGREDIENTS

- 1.5 lbs fresh mushrooms, sliced
- 1 large onion, diced
- 3 cloves garlic, minced
- 1 teaspoon dried thyme
- 1/2 teaspoon salt
- 1/4 teaspoon black pepper
- 1 cup beef broth
- 1 tablespoon Worcestershire sauce
- 1 cup sour cream (full fat)
- 2 tablespoons cream cheese (full fat)
- 1 tablespoon almond flour

Prep Time: 15 min

Cook Time: 6 hours

Serves: 4

DIRECTIONS

In the slow cooker, combine mushrooms, onion, garlic, thyme, salt, pepper, beef broth, and Worcestershire sauce. Stir to mix well. Cover and cook on low for 5-6 hours, until mushrooms are tender and flavors have melded. In a small bowl, mix the sour cream and cream cheese until smooth. If the stroganoff needs thickening, stir in almond flour into the sour cream mixture. Turn the slow cooker to high. Stir in the sour cream mixture into the mushrooms. Cover and cook for another 15-20 minutes until the sauce is thickened and creamy.

Serve garnished with fresh parsley. For a complete keto meal, serve over cauliflower rice or zucchini noodles.

NUTRITIONAL INFORMATION

Per serving: 280 calories, 8g protein, 10g carbohydrates, 24g fat, 2g fiber, 60mg cholesterol, 420mg sodium, 750mg potassium.

Crockpot Keto Vegetable Curry

INGREDIENTS

- 1 cauliflower, cut into florets
- 1 zucchini, sliced
- 1 bell pepper, sliced
- 1 cup green beans, trimmed
- 1 can (14 oz) coconut milk
- 2 tablespoons curry powder
- 1 teaspoon turmeric, cumin
- 1/2 teaspoon cayenne pepper (adjust to taste)
- 1 tablespoon ginger, minced
- 2 cloves garlic, minced
- 1 onion, diced

Prep Time: 15 min   Cook Time: **4 hours**   Serves: 4

DIRECTIONS

Place the cauliflower florets, zucchini slices, bell pepper slices, and green beans in the crockpot. In a bowl, whisk together the coconut milk, curry powder, turmeric, cumin, cayenne pepper, salt, and pepper until well combined. Stir in the minced ginger and garlic. Pour the coconut milk mixture over the vegetables in the crockpot, making sure everything is evenly coated. Sprinkle the diced onion on top. Cover and cook on low for 4 hours, until the vegetables are tender but not mushy. Stir the curry well before serving. Adjust seasoning if necessary. Serve hot, garnished with fresh cilantro.

NUTRITIONAL INFORMATION

Per serving: 220 calories, 5g protein, 15g carbohydrates, 17g fat, 6g fiber, 0mg cholesterol, 200mg sodium, 600mg potassium.

Slow Cooker Cheesy Cauliflower Casserole

INGREDIENTS

- 1 large head of cauliflower, cut into florets
- 1 cup heavy cream
- 1 cup shredded sharp cheddar cheese
- 1/2 cup grated Parmesan cheese
- 2 tablespoons cream cheese, softened
- 1 teaspoon garlic and onion powder
- 1/2 teaspoon mustard powder
- 1/4 cup almond flour
- 2 tablespoons unsalted butter, cut into small pieces

Prep Time: 15 min

Cook Time: 3 hours

Serves: 4

DIRECTIONS

Place cauliflower florets in the slow cooker. In a medium bowl, mix together heavy cream, cheddar cheese, Parmesan cheese, cream cheese, garlic powder, onion powder, mustard powder, salt, and pepper. Pour this mixture over the cauliflower, stirring to combine. In a small bowl, mix almond flour with butter pieces, creating a crumbly topping. Sprinkle this mixture over the cauliflower. Cover and cook on low for 3 hours, or until the cauliflower is tender and the sauce is bubbly. If desired, place the slow cooker insert under the broiler for a few minutes to brown the topping before serving. Watch carefully to prevent burning.

NUTRITIONAL INFORMATION

Per serving: 410 calories, 18g protein, 12g carbohydrates, 34g fat, 4g fiber, 105mg cholesterol, 500mg sodium, 450mg potassium.

Crockpot Spinach and Feta Quiche

INGREDIENTS

- 6 large eggs
- 1 cup heavy cream
- 1/2 teaspoon salt
- 1/4 teaspoon black pepper
- 1/2 teaspoon nutmeg
- 1 tablespoon olive oil
- 1 small onion, finely chopped
- 2 cloves garlic, minced
- 4 cups fresh spinach, roughly chopped
- 1 cup feta cheese, crumbled
- 1/4 cup grated Parmesan cheese

Prep Time: 15 minutes

Cook Time: 3 hours

Serves: 6

DIRECTIONS

In a large bowl, whisk together eggs, heavy cream, salt, pepper, and nutmeg. Set aside. Heat olive oil in a skillet over medium heat. Add onion and garlic, sautéing until softened. Add spinach and cook until wilted. Remove from heat and let cool slightly. Stir the spinach mixture into the egg mixture. Add feta and Parmesan cheeses, mixing until well combined. Pour the mixture into a greased slow cooker. Cover and cook on low for 2.5 to 3 hours, or until the center is set and edges are lightly golden. Let the quiche stand for 5 minutes before slicing. Serve warm.

NUTRITIONAL INFORMATION

Per serving: 320 calories, 18g protein, 5g carbohydrates, 26g fat, 1g fiber, 215mg cholesterol, 610mg sodium, 300mg potassium.

Slow Cooker Avocado Tex-Mex Soup

INGREDIENTS

- 1 pound chicken breasts, boneless and skinless
- 4 cups chicken broth (low sodium)
- 1 can (10 oz) diced tomatoes with green chilis, undrained
- 1 medium onion, chopped
- 2 cloves garlic, minced
- 1 teaspoon ground cumin
- 1 teaspoon chili powder
- 1/2 teaspoon paprika
- Salt and pepper to taste
- 1 large avocado, diced
- 1/2 cup fresh cilantro, chopped
- Juice of 1 lime

 Prep Time: 15 min   Cook Time: 6 hours   Serves: 4

DIRECTIONS

Place the chicken breasts at the bottom of the slow cooker. Add the chicken broth, diced tomatoes with green chilis, onion, garlic, cumin, chili powder, paprika, salt, and pepper. Stir to combine. Cover and cook on low for 6 hours or until the chicken is tender and can be easily shredded with a fork. Remove the chicken from the slow cooker, shred it using two forks, and then return it to the pot. Add the diced avocado, cilantro, and lime juice to the soup. Stir well to combine. Serve the soup hot, garnished with shredded cheddar cheese and a dollop of sour cream, if desired.

NUTRITIONAL INFORMATION

Per serving: 350 calories, 28g protein, 15g carbohydrates, 20g fat, 7g fiber, 75mg cholesterol, 700mg sodium, 800mg potassium.

Crockpot Butternut Squash Soup

INGREDIENTS

- 1 large butternut squash, peeled, seeded, and cut into cubes (about 6 cups)
- 1 medium onion, diced
- 2 cloves garlic, minced
- 4 cups vegetable broth (low sodium)
- 1 teaspoon ground cinnamon
- 1/2 teaspoon ground nutmeg
- 1/2 teaspoon ground ginger
- Salt and pepper to taste
- 1 cup coconut milk (for a creamy texture)

 Prep Time: 20 min   Cook Time: 6 hours   Serves: 4

DIRECTIONS

Combine butternut squash, onion, garlic, vegetable broth, cinnamon, nutmeg, ginger, salt, and pepper in the slow cooker. Stir well. Cover and cook on low for 6 hours until squash is tender. Use an immersion blender to puree the soup until smooth directly in the slow cooker. Alternatively, transfer to a blender, puree in batches, and return to the slow cooker. Stir in coconut milk until well combined. Adjust seasoning with salt and pepper. Heat through for an additional 10 minutes on low. Serve hot, garnished with roasted pumpkin seeds, a drizzle of coconut cream, and fresh herbs if desired.

NUTRITIONAL INFORMATION

Per serving: 250 calories, 4g protein, 30g carbohydrates, 14g fat, 5g fiber, 0mg cholesterol, 300mg sodium, 800mg potassium.

Slow Cooker Eggplant Parmesan

INGREDIENTS

- 2 large eggplants, sliced into 1/2 inch rounds
- 1 teaspoon salt (for sweating eggplant)
- 2 cups marinara sauce (low carb, sugar-free)
- 2 cups shredded mozzarella cheese
- 1 cup grated Parmesan cheese
- 1/2 cup almond flour
- 1/4 cup olive oil
- 2 teaspoons Italian seasoning
- 1 teaspoon garlic powder
- Salt and pepper to taste

Prep Time: 20 min

Cook Time: 4 hours

Serves: 4

DIRECTIONS

Lay the eggplant slices out and sprinkle with salt. Let them sit for about 10 minutes to sweat out bitterness, then pat dry with paper towels. In a bowl, mix almond flour, Italian seasoning, garlic powder, salt, and pepper. Lightly brush each eggplant slice with olive oil, then dredge in the almond flour mixture. In the slow cooker, spread a thin layer of marinara sauce. Layer eggplant slices, followed by a sprinkle of mozzarella and Parmesan cheeses. Repeat the layers until all ingredients are used, ending with cheese on top. Cover and cook on low for 4 hours, or until the eggplant is tender and the cheese is bubbly. Garnish with fresh basil before serving, if desired.

NUTRITIONAL INFORMATION

Per serving: 390 calories, 22g protein, 18g carbohydrates, 27g fat, 8g fiber, 55mg cholesterol, 790mg sodium, 750mg potassium.

Crockpot Zucchini and Yellow Squash Casserole

INGREDIENTS

- 2 medium zucchini, sliced
- 2 medium yellow squash, sliced
- 1 cup heavy cream
- 1 cup shredded mozzarella cheese
- 1/2 cup grated Parmesan cheese
- 2 tablespoons butter, cut into small pieces
- 1 teaspoon garlic powder
- 1 teaspoon onion powder
- Salt and pepper to taste
- 1/4 cup almond flour
- 2 tablespoons cold butter, cubed

Prep Time: 15 min   Cook Time: 4 hours   Serves: 4

DIRECTIONS

In the slow cooker, layer the sliced zucchini and yellow squash. Season each layer with salt, pepper, garlic powder, and onion powder. Pour the heavy cream over the squash layers. Sprinkle with mozzarella and Parmesan cheeses, then dot with the 2 tablespoons of butter. In a small bowl, combine the almond flour with the 2 tablespoons of cubed cold butter, using your fingers to mix until it forms a crumbly texture. Sprinkle this mixture over the top of the cheese. Cover and cook on low for 4 hours, or until the vegetables are tender and the top is slightly golden. Let the casserole stand for about 5 minutes before serving to allow the sauce to thicken slightly.

NUTRITIONAL INFORMATION

Per serving: 410 calories, 14g protein, 10g carbohydrates, 36g fat, 3g fiber, 105mg cholesterol, 320mg sodium, 500mg potassium.

Slow Cooker Tomato and Eggplant Stew

INGREDIENTS

- 1 large eggplant, cut into 1-inch cubes
- 2 cans (14.5 oz each) diced tomatoes, undrained
- 1 onion, chopped
- 3 cloves garlic, minced
- 1 bell pepper, diced
- 2 zucchinis, sliced
- 1/4 cup olive oil
- 1 teaspoon dried basil
- 1 teaspoon dried oregano
- Salt and pepper to taste

Prep Time: 15 min   Cook Time: 6 hours   Serves: 4

DIRECTIONS

Place the eggplant, diced tomatoes, onion, garlic, bell pepper, and zucchini in the slow cooker. Drizzle with olive oil and sprinkle with dried basil, oregano, salt, and pepper. Stir to combine. Cover and cook on low for 6 hours, until the vegetables are tender and the flavors have melded together. Adjust the seasoning with additional salt and pepper if needed. Serve hot, garnished with fresh basil and grated Parmesan cheese if desired.

NUTRITIONAL INFORMATION

Per serving: 220 calories, 4g protein, 25g carbohydrates, 14g fat, 10g fiber, 0mg cholesterol, 300mg sodium, 800mg potassium.

Crockpot Cheesy Asparagus

INGREDIENTS

- 2 pounds asparagus, trimmed
- 1 cup heavy cream
- 1 cup shredded cheddar cheese
- 1/2 cup grated Parmesan cheese
- 2 cloves garlic, minced
- Salt and pepper to taste
- 1/4 teaspoon nutmeg (optional)
- 1 tablespoon olive oil

Prep Time: 10 min   Cook Time: 2 hours   Serves: 4

DIRECTIONS

Lightly grease the slow cooker with olive oil. Place the trimmed asparagus in the bottom. In a small saucepan, heat the heavy cream and garlic over medium heat until just simmering. Remove from heat and stir in the cheddar cheese, Parmesan cheese, salt, pepper, and nutmeg until the cheese is melted and the mixture is smooth. Pour the cheese mixture over the asparagus in the slow cooker. Cover and cook on low for 2 hours, or until the asparagus is tender but still slightly crisp. Serve warm, with additional cheese sprinkled on top if desired.

NUTRITIONAL INFORMATION

Per serving: 350 calories, 15g protein, 10g carbohydrates, 29g fat, 3g fiber, 100mg cholesterol, 500mg sodium, 400mg potassium.

Slow Cooker Creamy Pumpkin Soup

INGREDIENTS

- 1 (15 oz) can pumpkin puree (not pumpkin pie filling)
- 3 cups vegetable broth (low sodium)
- 1 cup coconut milk (full fat for keto)
- 1 small onion, diced
- 2 cloves garlic, minced
- 1 tablespoon olive oil
- 1 teaspoon ground cinnamon
- 1/2 teaspoon ground nutmeg
- 1/4 teaspoon ground ginger
- Salt and pepper to taste

 Prep Time: 15 min

 Cook Time: 6 hours

 Serves: 6

DIRECTIONS

In a skillet over medium heat, heat the olive oil and sauté the onion and garlic until soft and translucent, about 5 minutes. Transfer the sautéed onion and garlic to the slow cooker. Add the pumpkin puree, vegetable broth, coconut milk, cinnamon, nutmeg, ginger, salt, and pepper. Stir to combine. Cover and cook on low for 6 hours, allowing the flavors to meld together. Before serving, blend the soup using an immersion blender until smooth (or transfer to a blender in batches, then return to the slow cooker). Serve warm, drizzled with heavy cream and garnished with pumpkin seeds.

NUTRITIONAL INFORMATION

Per serving: 180 calories, 3g protein, 14g carbohydrates, 14g fat, 4g fiber, 20mg cholesterol, 300mg sodium, 400mg potassium.

Crockpot Low-Carb Ratatouille

INGREDIENTS

- 1 large eggplant, cut into 1/2-inch pieces
- 2 medium zucchinis, sliced into 1/2-inch rounds
- 2 bell peppers (any color), chopped
- 1 large onion, chopped
- 3 cloves garlic, minced
- 1 can (28 ounces) diced tomatoes, drained
- 1/4 cup olive oil
- 2 tablespoons balsamic vinegar (check for sugar content for keto)
- 1 teaspoon dried thyme, oregano

 Prep Time: 20 minutes

 Cook Time: 4 hours

 Serves: 6

DIRECTIONS

In the slow cooker, combine the eggplant, zucchinis, bell peppers, onion, and garlic. Pour the diced tomatoes over the vegetables. In a small bowl, whisk together the olive oil, balsamic vinegar, thyme, oregano, salt, and pepper. Pour this mixture over the vegetables in the slow cooker and stir to combine.
Cover and cook on low for 4 hours, or until the vegetables are tender. Serve warm, garnished with fresh basil if desired.

NUTRITIONAL INFORMATION

Per serving: 180 calories, 3g protein, 18g carbohydrates, 12g fat, 6g fiber, 0mg cholesterol, 300mg sodium, 750mg potassium.

Slow Cooker Spicy Black Bean Soup

INGREDIENTS

- 1 pound dry black beans, soaked overnight and drained
- 4 cups vegetable broth (low sodium)
- 2 cups water
- 1 medium onion, chopped
- 2 cloves garlic, minced
- 1 red bell pepper, chopped
- 1 jalapeño, seeded and minced
- 1 teaspoon ground cumin, chili powder
- 1/2 teaspoon smoked paprika
- Juice of 1 lime

Prep Time: 15 min

Cook Time: 8 hours

Serves: 4

DIRECTIONS

Place the soaked and drained black beans in the slow cooker. Add the vegetable broth, water, onion, garlic, red bell pepper, jalapeño, cumin, chili powder, smoked paprika, salt, and pepper. Cover and cook on low for 8 hours, or until the beans are tender. Use an immersion blender to puree the soup to your desired consistency, leaving some beans whole for texture if preferred.

Stir in the lime juice and adjust seasoning with salt and pepper if needed. Serve hot, garnished with fresh cilantro and a dollop of sour cream, if desired.

NUTRITIONAL INFORMATION

Per serving: 330 calories, 20g protein, 60g carbohydrates, 1.5g fat, 15g fiber, 0mg cholesterol, 200mg sodium, 1400mg potassium.

Crockpot Golden Cauliflower Soup

INGREDIENTS

- 1 large head cauliflower, cut into florets
- 1 medium onion, chopped
- 2 cloves garlic, minced
- 4 cups vegetable broth (low sodium)
- 1 cup canned coconut milk
- 1 teaspoon turmeric
- 1/2 teaspoon ground ginger
- 1/4 teaspoon cayenne pepper (adjust to taste)
- Salt and pepper to taste
- 2 tablespoons olive oil
- Fresh parsley for garnish (optional)
- Roasted pumpkin seeds for garnish (optional)

Prep Time: 15 min

Cook Time: **6 hours**

Serves: 4

DIRECTIONS

Place cauliflower florets, onion, and garlic in the slow cooker. Add the vegetable broth, ensuring the vegetables are well covered. Stir in turmeric, ground ginger, cayenne pepper, salt, and pepper. Drizzle olive oil over the top.

Cover and cook on low for 6 hours, or until the cauliflower is very tender. Use an immersion blender to puree the soup until smooth. Stir in the coconut milk and adjust seasoning as needed. Serve hot, garnished with fresh parsley and roasted pumpkin seeds if desired.

NUTRITIONAL INFORMATION

Per serving: 220 calories, 6g protein, 18g carbohydrates, 15g fat, 5g fiber, 0mg cholesterol, 300mg sodium, 600mg potassium.

Slow Cooker Vegetarian Stuffed Peppers

INGREDIENTS

- 4 large bell peppers, tops cut off and seeds removed
- 1 cup cauliflower rice, cooked
- 1 cup shredded mozzarella cheese
- 1/2 cup feta cheese, crumbled
- 1 (8 oz) can diced tomatoes, drained
- 1/4 cup black olives, sliced
- 1/4 cup red onion, finely chopped
- 2 cloves garlic, minced
- 1 teaspoon Italian seasoning
- Salt and pepper to taste
- 1/4 cup vegetable broth
- Fresh parsley, chopped (for garnish)

Prep Time: 20 min   Cook Time: 4 hours   Serves: 4

DIRECTIONS

In a large bowl, mix together cauliflower rice, mozzarella cheese, feta cheese, diced tomatoes, black olives, red onion, garlic, Italian seasoning, salt, and pepper until well combined. Stuff each bell pepper with the cauliflower rice mixture and place them upright in the slow cooker. Pour vegetable broth into the bottom of the slow cooker, around the peppers. Cover and cook on low for 4 hours, or until the peppers are tender. Garnish with fresh parsley before serving.

NUTRITIONAL INFORMATION

Per serving: 200 calories, 12g protein, 15g carbohydrates, 10g fat, 4g fiber, 30mg cholesterol, 400mg sodium, 500mg potassium.

Desserts

Slow Cooker Low-Carb Chocolate Lava Cake

INGREDIENTS

- 1 cup almond flour
- 1/3 cup cocoa powder
- 1/2 cup erythritol (or another low-carb sweetener)
- 2 teaspoons baking powder
- 1/4 teaspoon salt
- 4 tablespoons unsalted butter, melted
- 2 large eggs
- 1/2 cup unsweetened almond milk
- 1 teaspoon vanilla extract
- 1/2 cup dark chocolate chips (sugar-free)

 Prep Time: 15 min

 Cook Time: 2 hours

 Serves: 4

DIRECTIONS

Whisk almond flour, cocoa powder, erythritol, baking powder, and salt in a large mixing bowl. In another bowl, mix melted butter, eggs, almond milk, and vanilla extract. Combine wet and dry ingredients, mix until smooth. Grease slow cooker pot. Pour half of the batter into the slow cooker. Sprinkle dark chocolate chips evenly, cover with the remaining batter. Cook on low for 2 hours until edges are cooked but center is slightly gooey. Let the cake stand for 10 minutes after cooking before serving.

NUTRITIONAL INFORMATION

Per serving: 320 calories, 12g protein, 10g carbohydrates, 28g fat, 5g fiber, 120mg cholesterol, 300mg sodium, 200mg potassium.

Crockpot Pumpkin Cheesecake

INGREDIENTS

- 1 cup almond flour
- 3 tablespoons unsalted butter, melted
- 1 tablespoon erythritol
- 16 ounces cream cheese, softened
- 1/2 cup pumpkin puree
- 3/4 cup erythritol
- 2 large eggs
- 1 teaspoon vanilla extract, ground cinnamon
- 1/2 teaspoon ground nutmeg
- 1/4 teaspoon ground ginger, salt

Prep Time: 20 minutes

Cook Time: 2 hours

Serves: 6

DIRECTIONS

Mix almond flour, melted butter, and erythritol for the crust. Press into the bottom of a greased 7-inch springform pan. Set aside. Beat cream cheese and erythritol until smooth. Add pumpkin puree, eggs, vanilla extract, cinnamon, nutmeg, ginger, and salt. Beat until well combined. Pour the filling over the crust in the springform pan. Cover with foil. Place a trivet or metal rack in the slow cooker, add 1 cup of water. Put the springform pan on the trivet. Cover and cook on high for 2 hours until set but slightly jiggly. Turn off the slow cooker and let the cheesecake cool inside for 1 hour. Chill in the refrigerator for at least 4 hours, or overnight, before serving.

NUTRITIONAL INFORMATION

Per serving: 410 calories, 10g protein, 10g carbohydrates, 38g fat, 2g fiber, 150mg cholesterol, 340mg sodium, 200mg potassium.

Keto Slow Cooker Berry Cobbler

INGREDIENTS

- 2 cups mixed berries (such as raspberries, blackberries, and blueberries), fresh or frozen
- 1 cup almond flour
- 1/2 cup coconut flour
- 1/3 cup erythritol (or any low-carb sweetener)
- 1 teaspoon baking powder
- 1/4 teaspoon salt
- 1/2 cup unsalted butter, melted
- 2 large eggs
- 1 teaspoon vanilla extract
- 1/2 cup unsweetened almond milk

 Prep Time: 10 minutes

 Cook Time: 3 hours

 Serves: 4

DIRECTIONS

Place the mixed berries in the bottom of the slow cooker. In a mixing bowl, combine almond flour, coconut flour, erythritol, baking powder, and salt. In another bowl, whisk together melted butter, eggs, vanilla extract, and almond milk until smooth. Gradually add the wet ingredients to the dry ingredients, stirring until just combined. The batter will be thick. Spoon the batter over the berries in the slow cooker, spreading it out to cover the berries evenly. Cover and cook on low for 3 hours, or until the top is set and lightly golden. Serve warm, optionally with a dollop of keto-friendly whipped cream or a scoop of low-carb ice cream.

NUTRITIONAL INFORMATION

Per serving: 400 calories, 10g protein, 18g carbohydrates, 34g fat, 10g fiber, 130mg cholesterol, 220mg sodium, 200mg potassium.

Slow Cooker Cinnamon Pecan Custard

INGREDIENTS

- 4 large eggs
- 1 cup heavy cream
- 1/2 cup unsweetened almond milk
- 1/2 cup granulated erythritol (or another keto-friendly sweetener)
- 1 teaspoon vanilla extract
- 1 teaspoon ground cinnamon
- 1/2 cup chopped pecans
- A pinch of salt

 Prep Time: 15 min

 Cook Time: 3 hours

 Serves: 4

DIRECTIONS

In a large bowl, whisk together eggs, heavy cream, almond milk, erythritol, vanilla extract, cinnamon, and salt until well combined. Grease the inside of the slow cooker pot lightly with butter or non-stick spray. Pour the custard mixture into the slow cooker. Sprinkle chopped pecans evenly over the top.
Cover and cook on low for 3 hours, or until the custard is set and the center is no longer liquid. Let cool slightly before serving. Can be served warm or chilled.

NUTRITIONAL INFORMATION

Per serving: 470 calories, 9g protein, 44g fat, 4g carbohydrates, 2g fiber, 1g sugar, 190mg cholesterol, 170mg sodium.

Crockpot Coconut Chocolate Fudge

INGREDIENTS

- 1 cup coconut oil
- 1 cup unsweetened cocoa powder
- 1/2 cup almond butter (no sugar added)
- 3/4 cup erythritol (powdered, for smoothness)
- 1 teaspoon vanilla extract
- A pinch of salt
- Unsweetened shredded coconut (for topping)

Prep Time: 10 min

Cook Time: 2 hours

Serves: 6

DIRECTIONS

In the slow cooker, combine coconut oil, cocoa powder, almond butter, erythritol, vanilla extract, and a pinch of salt. Stir to mix slightly. Cover and cook on low for 2 hours, stirring occasionally to ensure the mixture is smooth and well combined. Once the mixture is smooth and fully combined, pour it into a lined baking dish or silicone molds. Sprinkle unsweetened shredded coconut over the top for added texture and flavor. Refrigerate until set, typically about 2-3 hours or until firm. Cut into squares or pop out of the molds. Store in an airtight container in the refrigerator.

NUTRITIONAL INFORMATION

Per serving: 360 calories, 4g protein, 8g carbohydrates, 36g fat, 4g fiber, 0mg cholesterol, 5mg sodium, 200mg potassium.

Slow Cooker Lemon Cheesecake

INGREDIENTS

- 1 1/2 cups almond flour (for the crust)
- 1/4 cup unsalted butter, melted (for the crust)
- 2 tablespoons erythritol (for the crust)
- 16 ounces cream cheese, softened
- 1/2 cup erythritol
- 2 large eggs
- 1/4 cup sour cream
- Zest of 1 lemon
- 2 tablespoons lemon juice
- 1 teaspoon vanilla extract

Prep Time: 20 min   Cook Time: **2 hours**   Serves: **4**

DIRECTIONS

Mix almond flour, melted butter, and 2 tablespoons erythritol in a bowl. Press into the bottom of a greased springform pan. Place in the freezer to set. Beat cream cheese and 1/2 cup erythritol until smooth. Add eggs one at a time, beating well. Mix in sour cream, lemon zest, lemon juice, and vanilla extract.

Pour filling over the crust in the springform pan. Cover the top with a paper towel and aluminum foil. Place the pan in the slow cooker, pour water around it about 1 inch deep. Cook on high for 2 hours until cheesecake is set. Turn off the slow cooker, let the cheesecake cool inside until room temperature, then refrigerate for at least 4 hours before serving.

NUTRITIONAL INFORMATION

Per serving: 560 calories, 14g protein, 12g carbohydrates, 52g fat, 3g fiber, 180mg cholesterol, 340mg sodium, 200mg potassium.

Crockpot Spiced Apple Crumble

INGREDIENTS

- 4 cups peeled and sliced zucchini (as an apple substitute)
- 1 tablespoon lemon juice
- 1/3 cup erythritol
- 1 teaspoon ground cinnamon
- 1/4 teaspoon ground nutmeg

For the topping:

- 1 cup almond flour
- 1/2 cup chopped pecans
- 1/4 cup unsweetened shredded coconut
- 1/4 cup erythritol
- 1/2 cup unsalted butter
- 1 teaspoon vanilla extract

Prep Time: 15 minutes

Cook Time: 3 hours

Serves: 4

DIRECTIONS

In a large bowl, combine the sliced zucchini with lemon juice, erythritol, cinnamon, and nutmeg. Mix well to coat the zucchini slices evenly. Transfer the zucchini mixture to the slow cooker. In a separate bowl, mix together the almond flour, chopped pecans, shredded coconut, erythritol, melted butter, and vanilla extract until a crumbly mixture forms. Sprinkle the crumbly topping evenly over the zucchini mixture in the slow cooker. Cover and cook on low for 3 hours, or until the zucchini is tender and the topping is golden brown. Serve warm, optionally with a dollop of keto-friendly whipped cream or a scoop of low-carb ice cream.

NUTRITIONAL INFORMATION

Per serving: 480 calories, 8g protein, 14g carbohydrates, 44g fat, 7g fiber, 60mg cholesterol, 30mg sodium, 300mg potassium.

Slow Cooker Chocolate Peanut Butter Cake

INGREDIENTS

- 1 cup almond flour
- 1/2 cup unsweetened cocoa powder
- 3/4 cup erythritol (or any low-carb sweetener)
- 1 teaspoon baking powder
- 1/4 teaspoon salt
- 4 large eggs
- 1/2 cup unsalted butter, melted
- 1/4 cup unsweetened almond milk
- 1 teaspoon vanilla extract
- 1/2 cup natural peanut butter (sugar-free)

Prep Time: 15 min

Cook Time: 2.5 hours

Serves: 4

DIRECTIONS

In a large bowl, whisk together almond flour, cocoa powder, erythritol, baking powder, and salt. Beat in eggs, melted butter, almond milk, and vanilla extract until the batter is smooth. Pour half of the batter into a greased slow cooker. Dollop half of the peanut butter over the batter, then cover with the remaining batter. Swirl the remaining peanut butter on top with a knife or a fork. Cover and cook on low for 2.5 hours, or until a toothpick inserted into the center comes out mostly clean. Let the cake cool for about 20 minutes before serving. Serve warm or at room temperature.

NUTRITIONAL INFORMATION

Per serving: 630 calories, 20g protein, 15g carbohydrates, 55g fat, 8g fiber, 230mg cholesterol, 400mg sodium, 300mg potassium.

Crockpot Vanilla Ricotta Dessert

INGREDIENTS

- 2 cups whole milk ricotta cheese
- 1/2 cup erythritol (or any low-carb sweetener)
- 2 large eggs
- 1 teaspoon vanilla extract
- Zest of 1 lemon (optional for added flavor)
- A pinch of salt
- Almond slices and fresh berries for garnish (optional)

 Prep Time: 10 minutes

 Cook Time: 2 hours

 Serves: 4

DIRECTIONS

In a large bowl, mix together the ricotta cheese, erythritol, eggs, vanilla extract, lemon zest (if using), and a pinch of salt until well combined and smooth. Grease the inside of the slow cooker lightly with butter or non-stick spray. Pour the ricotta mixture into the slow cooker. Cover and cook on low for 2 hours, or until the mixture is set and slightly golden around the edges. Turn off the slow cooker and allow the dessert to cool for about 30 minutes before transferring it to the refrigerator. Chill for at least 2 hours before serving. Serve chilled, garnished with almond slices and fresh berries if desired.

NUTRITIONAL INFORMATION

Per serving: 280 calories, 18g protein, 6g carbohydrates, 20g fat, 0g fiber, 160mg cholesterol, 180mg sodium, 200mg potassium.

Slow Cooker Berry Compote with Whipped Cream

INGREDIENTS

- 4 cups mixed berries (such as raspberries, blackberries, strawberries, and blueberries), fresh or frozen
- 1/4 cup erythritol (or any low-carb sweetener)
- 1 teaspoon vanilla extract
- 1/2 teaspoon lemon zest

For the whipped cream:

- 1 cup heavy cream
- 2 tablespoons erythritol (or any low-carb sweetener)
- 1/2 teaspoon vanilla extract

Prep Time: 10 min   Cook Time: 2 hours   Serves: 4

DIRECTIONS

Place the mixed berries, erythritol, vanilla extract, and lemon zest in the slow cooker. Stir gently to combine. Cover and cook on low for 2 hours, or until the berries are soft and the sauce has thickened slightly. Stir gently once or twice during cooking, if possible. About 15 minutes before serving, make the whipped cream. In a mixing bowl, combine heavy cream, erythritol, and vanilla extract. Whip using a hand mixer or stand mixer until stiff peaks form.

Serve the warm berry compote in bowls or glasses, topped with a generous dollop of whipped cream.

NUTRITIONAL INFORMATION

Per serving: 300 calories, 2g protein, 18g carbohydrates, 25g fat, 5g fiber, 85mg cholesterol, 30mg sodium, 200mg potassium.

Crockpot Keto Chocolate Chip Cookie Bars

INGREDIENTS

- 2 cups almond flour
- 1/2 cup erythritol (or another keto-friendly sweetener)
- 1 teaspoon baking powder
- 1/4 teaspoon salt
- 1/2 cup unsalted butter, melted
- 1 teaspoon vanilla extract
- 2 large eggs
- 1/2 cup sugar-free chocolate chips

Prep Time: 15 minutes

Cook Time: 2 hours

Serves: 6

DIRECTIONS

In a large bowl, mix together the almond flour, erythritol, baking powder, and salt. Stir in the melted butter, vanilla extract, and eggs until a dough forms. Fold in the sugar-free chocolate chips. Line the bottom of the slow cooker with parchment paper, and grease the sides lightly with butter or cooking spray. Spread the cookie dough evenly in the bottom of the slow cooker. Cover and cook on low for 2 hours, or until the edges are golden brown and the center is set. Turn off the slow cooker and let the cookie bars cool completely before lifting them out using the parchment paper. Slice into bars once cooled.

NUTRITIONAL INFORMATION

Per serving: 320 calories, 10g protein, 8g carbohydrates, 28g fat, 4g fiber, 85mg cholesterol, 220mg sodium, 100mg potassium.

Slow Cooker Almond Joy Cake

INGREDIENTS

- 1 cup almond flour
- 1/3 cup coconut flour
- 1/2 cup unsweetened cocoa powder
- 3/4 cup erythritol
- 1 teaspoon baking powder
- 1/2 teaspoon salt
- 4 large eggs
- 1/2 cup unsalted butter
- 1/2 cup unsweetened almond milk
- 1 teaspoon vanilla extract
- 1/2 cup unsweetened shredded coconut
- 1/2 cup chopped almonds
- 1/4 cup sugar-free chocolate chips

Prep Time: 15 min

Cook Time: 3 hours

Serves: 4

DIRECTIONS

In a large bowl, whisk together almond flour, coconut flour, cocoa powder, erythritol, baking powder, and salt. In another bowl, mix together eggs, melted butter, almond milk, and vanilla extract. Stir the wet ingredients into the dry ingredients until well combined. Fold in shredded coconut, chopped almonds, and chocolate chips. Grease the inside of the slow cooker with butter or non-stick spray. Pour the batter into the slow cooker and spread evenly. Cover and cook on low for 3 hours, or until a toothpick inserted into the center comes out clean. Let the cake cool for a few minutes before serving. Optionally, garnish with additional shredded coconut, almonds, and chocolate chips.

NUTRITIONAL INFORMATION

Per serving: 580 calories, 18g protein, 20g carbohydrates, 50g fat, 10g fiber, 220mg cholesterol, 300mg sodium, 400mg potassium.

Slow Cooker Peach Cobbler

INGREDIENTS

- 4 chayote squash, peeled, pitted, and sliced thinly
- 1/4 cup lemon juice
- 1/2 cup erythritol (or any low-carb sweetener), divided
- 1 teaspoon vanilla extract
- 1 teaspoon cinnamon, divided
- 1 cup almond flour
- 1/4 cup coconut flour
- 1/2 cup unsalted butter, melted
- A pinch of salt
- 1/2 cup chopped pecans (optional)

Prep Time: 20 minutes

Cook Time: 3 hours

Serves: 4

DIRECTIONS

Toss sliced chayote squash with lemon juice, 1/4 cup erythritol, vanilla extract, and 1/2 teaspoon cinnamon in a large bowl. Transfer to a greased slow cooker. In another bowl, mix almond flour, coconut flour, remaining 1/4 cup erythritol, 1/2 teaspoon cinnamon, a pinch of salt, and melted butter until crumbly. Stir in chopped pecans if using. Sprinkle the crumb mixture over the squash. Cover and cook on low for 3 hours until filling is tender and topping is golden. Let the cobbler cool before serving. Serve warm, optionally with keto-friendly whipped cream or ice cream.

NUTRITIONAL INFORMATION

Per serving: 380 calories, 8g protein, 20g carbohydrates, 32g fat, 10g fiber, 60mg cholesterol, 100mg sodium, 400mg potassium.

Slow Cooker Keto Chocolate Peanut Butter Pudding

INGREDIENTS

For the crust:

- 1 1/2 cups almond flour
- 1/4 cup unsalted butter, melted
- 2 tablespoons powdered erythritol

For the filling:

- 1 cup creamy peanut butter
- 8 ounces cream cheese, softened
- 1/2 cup powdered erythritol
- 1/4 cup unsweetened cocoa powder
- 2 large eggs
- 1 teaspoon vanilla extract
- 1 1/2 cups almond milk.

Prep Time: 15 minutes

Cook Time: 2 hours

Serves: 6

DIRECTIONS

Mix almond flour, melted butter, and powdered erythritol, pressing the mixture into the bottom of a greased slow cooker. In another bowl, blend peanut butter, cream cheese, powdered erythritol, cocoa powder, eggs, and vanilla extract until smooth. Gradually add almond milk, stirring continuously, and pour the peanut butter filling over the almond flour crust in the slow cooker. Cover and cook on low for 2 hours until the pudding sets. After cooking, let it cool before serving, either warm or refrigerated for a chilled dessert. Optionally, top with chopped peanuts and sugar-free whipped cream before serving.

NUTRITIONAL INFORMATION

Per serving: 420 calories, 12g protein, 9g carbohydrates, 38g fat, 3g fiber, 130mg cholesterol, 300mg sodium, 200mg potassium.

Crockpot Cinnamon Roll Casserole

INGREDIENTS

For the cinnamon rolls:

- 2 cups almond flour
- 1/4 cup coconut flour
- 1/4 cup erythritol (or any low-carb sweetener)
- 1 tablespoon baking powder
- 1/4 teaspoon salt
- 2 large eggs
- 1/4 cup unsalted butter, melted
- 2 tablespoons unsweetened almond milk
- 1 teaspoon vanilla extract
-

For the filling:

- 1/4 cup unsalted butter, melted
- 1/4 cup erythritol (or any low-carb sweetener)
- 2 tablespoons ground cinnamon

For the cream cheese frosting:

- 4 ounces cream cheese, softened
- 2 tablespoons unsalted butter, softened
- 1/4 cup erythritol (powdered, for smoothness)
- 1/2 teaspoon vanilla extract
- 2 tablespoons heavy cream (as needed for desired consistency)

 Prep Time: 20 minutes

 Cook Time: 2.5 hours

 Serves: 4

DIRECTIONS

In a bowl, mix together almond flour, coconut flour, erythritol, baking powder, and salt. In another bowl, whisk together eggs, melted butter, almond milk, and vanilla extract. Combine wet and dry ingredients to form a dough. Roll out between two pieces of parchment paper to about 1/4 inch thickness. For the filling, brush the dough with melted butter, then sprinkle evenly with erythritol and cinnamon. Roll the dough tightly, starting at one end, to form a log. Slice into 8 rolls. Place the rolls in a greased slow cooker. Cook on low for 2.5 hours, or until set and lightly golden. For the frosting, beat together cream cheese, butter, erythritol, vanilla extract, and heavy cream until smooth. Spread over the warm cinnamon rolls before serving.

NUTRITIONAL INFORMATION

Per serving: 600 calories, 18g protein, 20g carbohydrates, 52g fat, 10g fiber, 180mg cholesterol, 400mg sodium, 300mg potassium.

Measurement Conversion Charts

MEASUREMENT

Cup	Ounces	Milliliters	Tablespoons
8 cups	64 oz	1895 ml	128
6 cups	48 oz	1420 ml	96
5 cups	40 oz	1180 ml	80
4 cups	32 oz	960 ml	64
2 cups	16 oz	480 ml	32
1 cup	8 oz	240 ml	16
3/4 cup	6 oz	177 ml	12
2/3 cup	5 oz	158 ml	11
1/2 cup	4 oz	118 ml	8
3/8 cup	3 oz	90 ml	6
1/3 cup	2.5 oz	79 ml	5.5
1/4 cup	2 oz	59 ml	4
1/8 cup	1 oz	30 ml	3
1/16 cup	1/2 oz	15 ml	1

WEIGHT

Imperial	Metric
1/2 oz	15 g
1 oz	29 g
2 oz	57 g
3 oz	85 g
4 oz	113 g
5 oz	141 g
6 oz	170 g
8 oz	227 g
10 oz	283 g
12 oz	340 g
13 oz	369 g
14 oz	397 g
15 oz	425 g
1 lb	453 g

TEMPERATURE

Fahrenheit	Celsius
100 °F	37 °C
150 °F	65 °C
200 °F	93 °C
250 °F	121 °C
300 °F	150 °C
325 °F	160 °C
350 °F	180 °C
375 °F	190 °C
400 °F	200 °C
425 °F	220 °C
450 °F	230 °C
500 °F	260 °C
525 °F	274 °C
550 °F	288 °C

Made in the USA
Monee, IL
17 November 2024

70363307R00083